FAMILY LEADERSHIP

Qawamah

An Obligation to Fulfill
<u>Not</u> An Excuse to Abuse

DR. MOHAMED RIDA BESHIR

amana publications

First Edition 2009A.C./1430A.H.

Copyright © 2009A.C./1430 A.H.

amana publications
10710 Tucker Street
Beltsville, MD 20705-2223 USA
Tel. (301) 595-5999
Fax (301) 595-5888
E-mail: amana@igprinting.com
www.amana-publications.com

Library of Congress Cataloging-in-Publication Data

Beshir, Mohamed Rida.
  Family leadership (qawamah) : an obligation to fulfill not an excuse to abuse / Mohamed
Rida Beshir.
     p. cm.
  Includes bibliographical references.
  ISBN 978-1-59008-056-6
  1. Family--Relgious aspects--Islam. 2. Muslim families. 3. Domestic relations (Islamic
law) I. Title.
  BP188.18.F35B47 2009
  297.5'77--dc22

                                                          2009015785

Printed in the United States of America

International Graphics
10710 Tucker Street
Beltsville, MD 20705-2223
Tel. (301) 595-5999
Fax (301) 595-5888
E-mail: ig@igprinting.com
www.igprinting.com

Acknowledgements

I would like to express my sincere gratitude to my daughters *Amirah,* Hoda, Noha, and Sumaiya, and their husbands Mohamed, Mohamed, Mohamed, and Hossam as well as my wife Dr. Ekram for all the time and hard work they put into formulating real life examples related to the proper and improper use of *Qawamah*. May Allah SWT bless them all, accept their good deeds, keep them all on the Straight Path, and reward them with *Jannah insha'a Allah*. Particular thanks are due to our daughters Noha and Sumaiya for editing this book. We will be forever indebted to all of them for their gracious support and dedication to this work.

I would also like to express my deepest gratitude to Dr. Jerald Dirks for his valuable comments and feedback as well as for writing the foreword for this work.

I kindly request that every reader make *Du'a* for them.

Foreword

At a time when divorce rates are skyrocketing in some predominantly Muslim countries, when increasing numbers of Muslim wives are reportedly seeking protection at battered women's shelters in North America, and when traditional family values are under repeated assault from a predominantly secular society, Dr. Mohamed Rida Beshir's present volume provides a timely and needed discussion of family leadership (*Qawamah*) from an Islamic perspective.

The first half of the book focuses on understanding two key words, i.e., *Qawamah* and *Daraba*, both of which have been frequently misrepresented by non-Muslim Orientalists and both of which have been all too often misunderstood by Muslims. To remedy this situation, Dr. Beshir begins with a linguistic analysis of *Qawamah*. Methodically, he surveys dictionary definitions of the root word (*Qaam*) of *Qawamah*, reviews Qur'anic verses (4:34; 4:135; and 5:8) that use *Qawamah* in its plural form, summarizes the meanings to be gleaned from the 663 Qur'anic verses that include a derivative or cognate of *Qawamah*, and presents relevant information from Qur'anic commentaries and contemporary Muslim scholars on **Qur'an** 4:34, whose statement about *Qawamah* reads as follows in the translation of 'Abdullah Yusuf 'Ali.

> Men are the protectors and maintainers of women, because Allah has given the one more (strength) than the other, and because they support them from their means.

While *Qawamah* does mean "to be in charge of" and "to take care of," these meanings do not give the husband an arbitrary and capricious dictatorship over his wife. As noted in Dr. Beshir's thoughtful review, *Qawamah* also has secondary meanings that imply the concepts of fairness and justice, and thus *Qawamah* must be done in a manner that is fair, just, kind, gentle, and merciful. Further, it must be done at the right time, e.g., not at the end of a heated discussion. Additionally, the right exercise of *Qawamah* necessitates that the husband give meaningful and thoughtful consideration to his wife's consultation (*Shura*) about all issues facing the family. Finally, it should be noted that *Qawamah* is not an unconditional right held by the husband. **Qur'an** 4:34 does not say that Allah has given the husband more strength or advantage than the wife. Rather, it says that Allah has given the one more strength or advantage than the other. This distinction is important because, as noted by Dr. Beshir's review of Al-Aloosy and Assabony, in some cases the wife may actually be the marital partner with more advantage.

Likewise, **Qur'an** 4:34 indicates that husbands exercise *Qawamah* because "they support them (the wives) from their (the husbands') means." In this regard, Dr. Beshir references Al-Qortoby and Al-Qasemy as stating that husbands may lose their right to *Qawamah* if they do not adequately fulfill the requirement of supporting their wives from their own financial means. This consideration raises important questions regarding *Qawamah* in those many Muslim marriages in which the wife is working and is financially contributing to the family's support and maintenance. In such cases, to what extent has the husband's right to *Qawamah* been compromised or even forfeited? While the book leaves it to the reader to sort through such questions, it must nevertheless be concluded that *Qawamah* is a conditional right, not an unconditional right, of the husband.

It is most unfortunate that many translators of **Qur'an** 4:34 render the concept of *Daraba* similarly to that given in the following translation of 'Abdullah Yusuf 'Ali, where the concept is translated as "beat."

> As to those women on whose part ye fear disloyalty and ill-conduct, admonish them (first), (next), refuse to share their beds, (and last) beat them (lightly); but if they return to obedience, seek not against them means (of annoyance)...

In English, the words "beat them," however lightly that beating may be, suggest physical abuse and domestic violence. As Dr. Beshir strongly notes, there is no place for physical abuse and domestic violence within the confines of an Islamic marriage or within the boundaries of Islam. Nonetheless, social workers who staff women's safe houses have informed me on more than one occasion that Muslim husbands often attempt to justify their physical abuse of their wives by resorting to **Qur'an** 4:34, as though this verse gives them some sort of God-given right to abuse their wives. Such a perversion of the **Qur'an** is not to be tolerated, and Dr. Beshir is quick to condemn such an interpretation of **Qur'an** 4:34.

As Dr. Beshir illustrates by linguistic analysis, *Daraba* has multiple possible meanings, only one of which has to do with beating. Other possible meanings include strike, tap, expound, separate from, embrace sexually, etc., and the correct understanding of *Daraba* depends upon context. Given the multiple *Ahadith* referenced by Dr. Beshir, it is clear that *Daraba* in **Qur'an** 4:34 cannot mean beat. Further, Dr. Beshir's review of the literature suggests that there are three possible interpretations of *Daraba* in **Qur'an** 4:34. Firstly, *Daraba* may mean to tap lightly, for example with a toothbrush or folded handkerchief, in a way that causes no physical discomfort, that does not touch the face, and that is not done in public. In this understanding, *Daraba* indicates a private, strictly symbolic, and non-physically discomforting expression of displeasure, which functions almost like a marital psychodrama. Secondly, *Daraba* may mean to separate from one's wife, an understanding that is becoming more and more popular among contemporary scholars. Thirdly, it may mean to embrace sexually, either after a set period of refusing to share the wife's bed or after the wife amends her behavior. Under any of the three understandings, *Daraba* is never a license for causing any amount of physical pain or discomfort.

The second half of Dr. Beshir's book turns to practical application of *Qawamah* in contemporary Muslim marriages in North America. Here the reader is presented with numerous examples of family leadership being practiced by Muslim husbands. The first set of eight examples illustrates the appropriate use of *Qawamah*. The second set of nine examples highlights the inappropriate exercise of *Qawamah*. In both cases, Dr. Beshir presents an analysis of why the example is an appropriate or inappropriate expression of *Qawamah*. These examples are straight forward, easy to follow, and provide a practical illustration of the scholarly conclusions found in the first half of the book.

The present volume is not, and was not intended as, the final, be-all, end-all consideration of family leadership within an Islamic context. However, it is an extremely valuable springboard for further discussion and consideration of a most timely topic that affects every Muslim family in North America. As a Muslim with a doctorate in clinical psychology, it is my professional recommendation that every mosque and Islamic center in North America should use Dr. Beshir's new book to lead in-depth study and discussion sessions about the role of family leadership within Islam. In doing so, it is my hope that their discussions will not end at the boundaries of Dr. Beshir's book, but that they will utilize Dr. Beshir's book' to begin penetrating even deeper into the issue of family leadership, will consider and discuss their own examples of appropriate and inappropriate exercise of *Qawamah*, and will thereby strengthen their own families.

Jerald F. Dirks, M.Div., Psy.D.
May 1, 2009

Counseling many Muslim families has given us an in depth view regarding misconceptions about *Qawamah* in the minds of both husbands and wives. The misunderstandings about *Qawamah* cover a wide range of areas in the life of Muslim families. They vary from one extreme to the other. On one side of the spectrum, we have dealt with men who think that they have the right to boss their wives around and order them right and left, while the wife has no right to discuss or refuse any of her husband's requests. On the other side of the spectrum, we have dealt with ladies who have been greatly influenced by a negative feminist mentality and think that their husbands have no right to make a final decision related to their family matters, even if he has consulted with them and fulfilled all the requirements of *Qawamah*.

Our methodology in this work is to try to understand thoroughly the meaning of the word *Qawamah* from a linguistic point of view, by looking at the various authentic Arabic Dictionaries. This will help us to come up with various components that are included in the meaning of this very important concept. Next we will study and discuss the main verse in the **Qur'an** discussing the concept of *Qawamah*, which is verse number 34 in Surah number 4 (*Surah Al-Nisa'*). We will do this by surveying many of the Qur'anic interpretation references (*Tafaseer*) available in the Islamic library as well as some of the literature dealing with this concept. Of course, it is impossible to go over all *Tafaseers* and available written material about this important subject. As such, we will try to make sure that we cover some of the historically old and early *Tafaseers*, as well as some of the newer commentaries on the **Qur'an**. We will also try to make sure that we survey work done by interpreters from various geographical areas within the Muslim world and not to limit ourselves to only those of Arabic origin. We feel that this is important for the concept of *Qawamah*, because the understanding of the concept mutually affects and is being affected by the social life, culture, and traditions of the ethnic background.of the writer Also, in presenting various literature sources on the topic, we will try to avoid repeating the same ideas mentioned by commentators. Our goal is to capture as many views, thoughts, and opinions as possible from diverse sources.

The results of the above linguistic surveys and *Tafaseers* leads us to a concise and very clear understanding of the concept of *Qawamah*.

However, a concept stays abstract if not augmented by practical examples, particularly with such a misunderstood one as *Qawamah*; it stays intangible in the mind of the reader. Our goal is to make sure that our readers understand the concept of *Qawamah* properly and know clearly its applications in various areas of their lives. As such, we have devoted the last two chapters of this book to practical examples in order to illustrate the proper and improper use of this significant concept. These realistic examples cover a variety of actual life situations, and we feel they will help our readers greatly comprehend and appreciate the depth of the *Qawamah* concept and realize the breadth of its application in the life of a Muslim family.

We divided these practical examples into two categories. In both categories, we provided examples related to the early stage of marriage, to life after few years of marriage, and to a very mature marriage where the couple has been married for many years and are blessed with many children.

The first category describes the appropriate use of *Qawamah*. It covers a wide variety of situations, including a couple in the early stage of marriage where the wife is still finishing her studies, a married couple who have different views about the wife applying for a job, the family moving from an environment that is familiar for the wife in order for the husband to pursue better career opportunities, a wife who wants to visit her family every summer because she misses them; and a couple who disagree on the amount of money they should donate to save the town mosque.

Family Leadership (Qawamah)

The second category deals with the inappropriate use of *Qawamah*. It covers diverse family situations, such as a husband who does not allow his wife to travel alone to visit her elderly parents, even though there is a safe trip available with no stopover; a husband refusing to allow his wife to work in her field of specialization without discussing the reasons although they have no children, a husband marrying a second wife without informing his first wife; a husband who is not willing to accommodate the needs of his wife's Islamic education via a sisters study circle at their place; a husband who doesn't want to share a small portion of helping the children with their homework, and who expects his wife to carry the full load of house chores even though they both work full time and he has agreed to this; and a husband who doesn't want to make any time for his wife and children to visit relatives on weekends.

One of the worst misconceptions with regards to *Qawamah* is linking it to domestic violence by citing the famous quranic verse we referred to earlier (verse 34 in chapter 4). This link is sometimes made by orientalists, as well as Muslim men who don't understand the verse properly and are using it to justify their ill behaviour towards their wives. Let us make it absolutely clear that there is no place in Islam for domestic violence. Prophet Muhammad *SAAW* condemned this practice very clearly in many of his teachings.

Husbands who think that this verse gives them the right to deal with their wives in a violent way or to settle conflicts by striking or beating their wives are completely ignorant of Islamic teachings as they relate to family life. They are not true followers of Prophet Muhammad *SAAW* but are rather extremely misguided in their understanding of this verse. He, the Prophet *SAAW*, is innocent of their unacceptable deeds.

Available statistics on domestic violence among Muslim families indicate that husbands act violently against their wives in a fit of rage and usually resort to violence as the first tool to resolve the conflict at hand. This is completely unacceptable from an Islamic point of view and is strongly condemned by Muslim scholars, leaders, and community activists alike.

Introduction

A Note about the Writing

Italicized fonts refer to Arabic names or common Arabic terminology used by Muslims.

The use of (Q j, V i) denotes that this reference is the ith verse from the jth chapter in the **Qur'an**. For example, (Q 2, V 7) denotes the 7th verse in the 2nd chapter of the **Qur'an.**

There are six major books referring to the collections of sayings (*Hadeeth*) of the prophet PBUH. These books are *Bukhari, Muslim, Abu Dawoud, An-Nisa'ee, At-Termithy,* and *Ibn Majah.* After a hadeeth, the names in footnote refer to which book the *Hadeeth* was taken from. When the expression Agreed upon appears in the footnote, it means that this *Hadeeth* is reported by both *Bukhari* and *Muslim.*

When the abbreviation *SAAW* is used, usually after the name of Prophet Muhammad, it stands for "may Allah's peace and blessings be upon him." When the abbreviation *RAA* is used, usually it is after the name of one of the companions of the Prophet *SAAW* who narrated his sayings, it means "may Allah be pleased with him."

Dr. Mohamed Rida Beshir

Contents

ACKNOWLEDGEMENTS iii

FOREWORD iv

INTRODUCTION viii

WHAT IS *QAWAMAH* 1

    • Introduction   1

    • Meaning of *Qawamah*   1

  1. IN DICTIONARIES   1

    • *Al Mesbah Al Muneer*   1

    • *Al-Saheeh Fi Alloghah Wal Oloom*   2

    • *Al Qamoos Al Muheet*   2

    • *Lesan Al-Arab*   2

    • *Moheet al Moheet*   3

    • *Qur'anic Keywords; A Reference Guide*   3

  2. From Qur'anic verses   5

    • The Meaning of *Qawamah*: Summary based on dictionaries
      and use of word in the ***Qur'an***   7

    • *Qawamah* in the ***Qur'an***   8

    • English translation of the verse   9

    – Muhammad Asad   9

    – Dr. Mohammad Mohsen Khan and
       Dr. Mohammad Taqi-ud-din Al Hilali   10

INTERPRETATION OF THE *QAWAMAH* VERSE 14

    • Introduction   14

    • General interpretation of the verse   15

    – Al-Fakhr Al-Razy   16

Contents

– Al-Qortoby   16

– Al Aloosy   17

– Sheikh Muhammad Ali Assabony Comment   17

– *Fi Zelal Al Qur'an*   18

– *Mahasen Al-Ta'weel*   20

– *Tafheem ul Qur'an*   21

– A. Yusuf Ali Commentary   21

– *Al-Tafseer Al-Muneer*   22

– Sh. Muhammad Al-Ghazaly Commentary   23

– Sh. Muhammad Metwally Al-Sha'rawy Commentary   23

– Mohamed Asad's Commentary   25

– *The Fragile Vessels*   27

– Ahmed Ali's Comment   27

– Dr. Abdelhameed Abusulayman   28

– Ustaz Abdel Haleem Abu Shoqah   30

– Dr. Saalih ibn Ghaanim Al-Sadlaan   32

– Dr. Jerald F. Firks Commentary   33

PROPER UNDERSTANDING OF THE *QAWAMAH* CONCEPT **36**

• *Qawamah*, Important concept to be understood   36

• *Qawamah*, a responsibility and obligation to be fulfilled   38

• *Taqwa* of Allah *SWT*   39

• Proper understanding of the real meaning of *Qawamah*   39

• Good manners   40

• *Qawamah* and domestic violence   40

APPROPRIATE USE OF *QAWAMAH* **49**

• Introduction   49

• Campus Calls   49

– Why it is Appropriate   50

• When it Rains it Pours   50

– Why it is Appropriate   51

• The Dead End Job   52

– Why it is Appropriate   53

• Hajj is in the Air   54

– Why it is appropriate   55

• One Car is Better than Two   55

– Why it is Appropriate   57

• Any Plans?   57

– Why it is Appropriate   60

• Looking Good…Too Good   60

– Why it is Appropriate   61

• I Want my Mommy   61

– Why it is Appropriate   62

INAPPROPRIATE USE OF QAWAMAH 63

• Introduction   63

• I have made my Decision, End of Discussion   63

– Why it is Inappropriate   64

• There is Nothing more to Discuss   64

– Why it is Inappropriate   65

• That is Impossible, I am his Wife   65

– Why it is Inappropriate   66

• I would Just like to be Able to Come Home
  to a Quiet House and Relax   66

– Why it is Inappropriate   67

Contents

• Double Duty, Single Effort   68

– Why it is Inappropriate   69

• You are not Going. It is your Duty to Obey   69

– Why it is Inappropriate   70

• I am a Person Too!   71

– Why it is Inappropriate   72

• What were you Doing All Day?   73

– Why it is Inappropriate   75

• Story of my Life   76

– Why it is Inappropriate   79

ARABIC TERMINOLOGY 81

• Introduction   81

• Glossary of Arabic terms   81

REFERENCES 90

What Is *Qawamah*

I n this chapter our emphasis will be on the linguistic meaning of the word *Qawamah* and we will try our best to present the proper understanding of *Qawamah*. We will do this through using various linguistic tools such as the Arabic meanings of the root of the word Qawamah as it appears in some of the most authentic Arabic dictionaries, such as *Mukhtar Al Sahas, Al Misbah Al Muneer, Al-Qamoos Al-Muheet,* etc. We will also try to help the reader comprehend and appreciate the con- cept of *Qawamah* via two approaches. The first is by enlisting and explain- ing some of the Qur'anic verses that include the word *Qawamah* or many of its derivatives, and the second is by sifting through a great number of Qura'nic interpretations (Tafaseer) such as *Tafseer Ibn Katheer, Al-Jame' Le-Ahkam Al-Qur'an, Tafhum ul Quràn, Fi Zelal Al-Qur'an,* etc. For the sake of completion we will also quote the views of some of our Muslim scholars regarding this subject. At the end of this chapter, we will conclude with a concise definition of *Qawamah* in Islam, taking into consideration the Arabic meaning of the word as well as the views of various Qur'anic interpreters (*Mufassereen*). This second part will be done in a later chapter *inshaà Allah.*

MEANING OF QAWAMAH

1. IN DICTIONARIES

Al Misbah Al Muneer

According to the Arabic dictionary *Al Misbah Al-Muneer,* page 714, under the explanation of the word *Qawm*, it indicates that the root word is *Qaam* and it means to take care of. It continues to describe a person who takes care of something with the word *Qawwaam*. When the word is *Qewam*, it means the provision or the food that supports humans. When it is **Qawam** it means just and fair. The word **Qawm** means a group of people including men and women. They are called *Qawm* because they take care of those who live with them. They provide the support needed in various aspects of life to the members of their group, particularly security and protection, where individuals may not be able to do it alone. The word *Aqaam* means to establish and make something superior and recognized as such. As in *Aqaam Al-Salat* which means to establish regular prayers or *Aqaam Al-Share'* which means to establish rules and regulations according to **Qur'an** and the teachings of Prophet Muhammad *SAAW*.[1]

Al-Saheeh Fi Alloghah Wal Oloom

According to the Arabic dictionary **Al-Saheeh Fi Alloghah Wal Oloom**[2], page 965-967, similar explanations are given for the word *Qawm*. It also adds that "*Alqawam*" means a person who is just.

Al Qamoos Al Moheet

As for the Arabic dictionary **Al Qamoos Al Moheet**[3] similar explanations for the word **Qawm** and *Qawamah* are discussed with great emphasis on the element of protection for *Qawm* and on the elements of being just and upright for a person who is given the state of *Qawamah*.

Lesan Al Arab

According to the Arabic dictionary **Lesan Al Arab**[4], pages 503-506, a very similar explanation is given to the word *Qawm*. It adds that a Qayemah Mellah is the moderate way. The *Qayemah Mellah* also carries the connotation of being excellent, straight, and upright. It indicates that

---

[1] Al Alammah Ahmad Ibn Muhammad Ibn Aly Almaqry Al faiomy. **Ketab AlMesbah Al Muneer Fi Ghareeb Al Sharh Al Kabeer,** Part 1 and 2, Six edition, Al-Matbah Al Amereiah, Cairo, 1925

[2] Nadeem Mara'shly and Osama Mara'shly, **Al-Saheeh Fi Alloghah Wa Aloloom,** Dar Alhadarah Al-Arabiah, Beirut, first edition, 1975

[3] Majd Al Deen Al Fayrooz Abady, **Al Qamoos al Moheet,** Volume 3 page 168, Al-sa'adah Print house, Egypt, 1913, 1332H

[4] Aby Al Fadl Jamal al Deen Muhammad Ibn Makram Ibn Manzoor Al-Afriqey Al-Masry, **Lesan al Arab,** Volume 12, Sader House for printing and Publications, Beirut, 1956, 1375H

the same root of the word *Qawm* is used for one of the most beautiful names of Allah *SWT*, *Al-Qayoom*, which means The One Who is in full charge of His creation and their provision and has full knowledge of everything. It also means the One Who is in charge of everything. The dictionary also touches upon another very important meaning for another word that shares the same root, which is *Qewam*. It indicates that it means the provisions and various needed foods and commodities that a person can't live without. Another important word that shares the same root is *Oqawem* which means to resist giving up and to struggle to fulfill duties. Further to this, it discusses the word *Maqam*, which means the place of dwelling or the place a person or a group uses to meet and discuss their affairs, or simply to socialize.

Moheet Al Moheet

As for the Arabic dictionary **Moheet Al Moheet** [5], it emphasizes that a *Qawwam* person is one who is just, is fair, and does what it takes to provide his family with the adequate means needed for them to live a dignified life. This person strives hard to be upright and moderate. This person also takes good care of his family from a religious perspective, by teaching them their religious duties and helping them to be closer to Allah and live according to His guidance.

Qur'anic Keywords: A Reference Guide

According to **Qur'anic Keywords; A Reference Guide** [6], Abdur Rasheed Siddiqui states the following under the meaning of **Iqamah** (Establishment):

"**Iqamah** is from *Qama*, meaning to get up, to stand up or to stand erect. Hence *Iqamah* means raising, lifting up, elevation, sitting up, erection, or establishment (of something). The essence of *Iqamah* is to

---

[5] Al Mo'alem Botros al Bostany, *Qamoos Motawwal for Arabic Language; Moheet al Moheet*, Maktabat Lobnan, Reyad al Solh square, Beirut, 1987
[6] Abdur Rasheed Sidddiqui, *Qur'anic Keywords, A Reference Guide*, The Islamic Foundation, United Kingdom, 2008 PP 112-114

make something stand in such a way that it is not bent or crooked. When *Iqamah* is used of an abstract thing, it means to establish an apparatus for it to function properly. For example, it is extensively used for establishing prayers. The word *Iqamah* is also used for staying or residing somewhere."

It is instructive to note that the instruction in the **Qur'an** is always *Aqimu al-Salat* (establish prayer) not just "pray". *Iqamah* is a comprehensive term. It does not mean that one should pray regularly and individually but that there should be a collective provision established for offering prayers. There should be a definite place of worship (mosque), facilities for *Wudu*, organization of *Adhan*, appointment of an Imam, and arrangement of Jumu'ah prayers and *Khutbahs*. Even standing straight in rows, according to one *hadith*, is part of *Iqamat al-Salah*. The *Iqamah* to alert worshippers (whose wording is similar to the *Adhan* with the addition of *qad qamat as-Salah*) is said when prayer is ready to be performed, and people within the mosques get ready and form rows.

Iqamat al-Din is the other frequent usage of this term in the **Qur'an**. It implies that the whole system of *Din* should be established in one's own life as well as collectively in society. As *al-Din* embraces all aspects of life, its *Iqamah* requires that it is followed diligently as much as possible in one's life and in the life of the Muslim community.

Many words derived from the word *Qama* occur in the **Qur'an**. The *Qiyam* is the standing posture in **Salah**. The word *Qiyam* is also used to convey other meanings: The *Qiyam al-Layl* means standing up in prayers at night and reciting **Qur'an**. It generally means to stay up for the whole or part of the night performing acts of *'ibadah*. It was compulsory for the Prophet *SAAW*[7] but other Companions also joined in the *Qiyam*. *Qiyam al-Layl* in *Ramadan* is the prescribed tarawih prayers and performance of other acts of *'Ibadah* during the night especially during the last ten nights of *Ramadan*.

---

[7] (Q73, V2-4, V20)

The *Qawwam* means the provider or supporter, manager, caretaker, guardian, or custodian. This word is used in *Surat al-Nisa'*, verse 34 and it means that men are guardians and protectors of their womenfolk.

Al-Qayyum is one of the most beautiful names (*al-Asmaa' al- Husna*) of Allah, which means He is the One Who is Self Subsisting, the Everlasting or the Eternal.

Qiyamah or *Yawm al-Qiyamah* is the day when the dead will be raised from their graves and all of them will stand up before Allah.

Istiqamah means uprightness, sincerity, integrity, steadfastness or firmness. This is a desirable quality of believers. It means that they remain steadfast in their *Iman*.[8] The key to *Istiqamah* is to remain upright and steadfast facing all difficulties and hardship. This can only be achieved if one's heart is full of firm *Iman* and is devoid of any doubt. Imam Ghazali stated that the importance and need for *Istiqamah* is so great that Allah *SWT* has ordered the recitation of *Surah al Fatihah*, where there is a supplication of *Istiqamah* or continuous guidance to the straight path.

2. FROM QUR'ANIC VERSES:

The word *Qawwam* appears in three locations in **Qur'an**. In all of them it appears in the plural (*Qawwamoon* and *Qawwameen*) and not the singular form. These are:

"Men are *Qawwamoon* on women with the bounties that God has bestowed more abundantly on the former than on the latter, and with that they may spend out of their possessions. And the righteous women are the truly devout ones, who guard the intimacy that God has [ordained to be] guarded. As for those women whose ill-will you have reason to fear, admonish them [first]; then leave them alone in bed; then beat them; and if thereupon they pay you heed, don't seek to harm them. Behold, God is indeed most high, great."[9]

---

[8] (Q41, V30 and Q46, V13)

[9] (Q4, V34)

5

"Believers! Be *Qawwameen* of Justice, and bearers of witness to truth for the sake of Allah, even though it may either be against yourselves or against your parents and kinsmen, or the rich or the poor: for Allah is more concerned with their well-being than you are. Don't then follow your own desires lest you keep away from justice. If you twist or turn away from the truth, know that Allah is well aware of what you do."[10]

"Believers; be *Qawwameen* (stand out firmly) for Allah, as just witnesses; and let not the enmity of others make you avoid justice. Be just: that is near to piety; and fear Allah. Verily Allah is Well-Acquainted with what you do."[11]

Other words that come from the same root as the word *Qawwam* appear in the **Qur'an** in 663 places. 383 of them are related to the word "*Qawm*" such as *Al-Qawm, Qawmy, Qawman, Qawmak*, etc. The word *Qawm* means, as indicated earlier, a group of people including men and women who share the same habitat. They are called *Qawm* because they take care of those who live with them. 77 instances are of the word "*Al-Qeiamah*" which means "The Day of Resurrection." 47 instances are related to the word "*Al-Mostaqeem*" and other words such as *Estaqamo, Yastaqeem, Estaqem, Estaqeema*, and *Estaqeemo* which more or less means to be straight and upright. The rest of the words are *Qama* and the like, *Aqoomo* and the like, *Maqam* and the like, *Al-Qaiyoom*, etc. Following are these verses that could shed more light on the meaning of *Qawamah*:

"The lightning almost snatches away their sight, whenever it flashes for them, they walk therein, and when darkness covers them *Qamoo* (they stand still.) And if Allah willed, He could have taken away their hearing and their sight. Certainly, Allah has power over all things."[12]

---

[10] (Q4, V135)

[11] (Q5, V8)

[12] (Q2, V20)

6

"Allah, there is no god but Him, the Ever living, *Al-Qayoom* (the One Who sustains and protects all that exists). Neither slumber nor sleep overtakes Him. To Him belongs whatever is in the heavens and whatever is on the earth. Who is he who can intercede with Him except with His permission? He knows what happens to them (His creatures) in this world and what will happen to them in Hereafter. And they will never compass anything of His knowledge except that which He wills. His *Kursi* (throne) extends over the heavens and the earth, and He feels no fatigue in guarding and preserving them. And He is the Most High, the Most Great."[13]

"Men are *Qawwamoon* over women with the bounties that God has bestowed more abundantly on the former than on the latter, and with that they may spend out of their possessions. And the righteous women are the truly devout ones, who guard the intimacy that God has [ordained to be] guarded. As for those women whose ill-will you have reason to fear, admonish them [first]; then leave them alone in bed; then beat them; and if there-upon they pay you heed, don't seek to harm them. Behold, God is indeed most high, great."[14]

"Say (O Muhammad *SAAW*) Truly, my Lord has guided me to a Straight Path, a religion that is *Qiyaman* (a right religion,) the way of Ibraheem Hanifan (the true Islamic monotheist, who believed in one God, Allah, and worshipped none but Him Alone) and he was not of the disbelievers."[15]

The Meaning of *Qawamah*: Summary based on dictionaries and the use of the word in the *Qur'an*

From the above discussions of the authentic dictionaries, as well as

---

[13] (Q2, V255)

[14] (Q4, V34)

[15] (Q6, V161)

verses of *Qur'an*, we can say that *Qawamah* means family leadership or guardianship. It covers and encompasses a wide spectrum of qualities and meanings that can contain at least the following elements:

- Carrying responsibility and trust
- Taking care of or caring for
- Protecting and safeguarding
- Maintaining
- Supporting
- Providing
- Offering family leadership
- Helping and assisting
- Cooperating
- Coaching, mentoring, and guiding
- Consulting and counselling
- Providing security and safety
- Managing the affairs of
- Administrating and supervising
- Bringing good values to the relationship

QAWAMAH IN QUR'AN

The main verse talking about *Qawamah* in **Qur'an** is verse number 34 in the 4th chapter entitled 'WOMEN' "*Surah Al-Nesa.*" The Arabic text of the verse reads as follow:

ٱلرِّجَالُ قَوَّامُونَ عَلَى ٱلنِّسَاءِ بِمَا فَضَّلَ ٱللَّهُ بَعْضَهُمْ عَلَىٰ بَعْضٍ وَبِمَا أَنفَقُوا مِنْ أَمْوَالِهِمْ فَٱلصَّالِحَاتُ قَانِتَاتٌ حَافِظَاتٌ لِّلْغَيْبِ بِمَا حَفِظَ ٱللَّهُ وَٱلَّاتِى تَخَافُونَ نُشُوزَهُنَّ فَعِظُوهُنَّ وَٱهْجُرُوهُنَّ فِى ٱلْمَضَاجِعِ وَٱضْرِبُوهُنَّ فَإِنْ أَطَعْنَكُمْ فَلَا تَبْغُوا عَلَيْهِنَّ سَبِيلًا إِنَّ ٱللَّهَ كَانَ عَلِيًّا كَبِيرًا

English Translations of the Verse

After, reviewing various available translations of the verse in the literature while focusing on the two key Arabic words most relevant to this research; *Qawwamoon* and *Udhdhribuuhon*, we can conclude the following:

1. *Qawwamoon* is translated to the following in English:

    a. Taking full care of

    b. The protectors and maintainers of

    c. Overseers over

    d. Should take full care of

    e. The supporters of

    f. In charge of

    g. The ones who should support

    h. Made responsible for

    i. Have charge of

    j. The support of

2. *Udhdhribuuhon* is translated to the following in English

    a. Beat or hit them in a gentle manner or lightly. Some scholars prefer to use the word strike instead of beat or hit, as we will see in the detailed interpretation of the verse in a later chapter[16]

    b. Distance yourself from them[17]

    c. Have sexual intercourse with them[18]

Here are a few examples of translations of the full verse which highlight the meanings listed above:

Muhammad Asad

In his book, ***The Message of the Qur'an*** [19] Muhammad Asad translates the verse as follows:

---

[16] See reference 61 for this example
[17] See reference 27 as an example
[18] See reference 19 as an example
[19] Mohammad Asad, ***The message of the Qur'an Translated and Explained***, Dar Al-Andalus, Gibraltar

"MEN SHALL take full care of women with the bounties which God has bestowed more abundantly on the former than on the latter, and with that they may spend out of their possessions. And the righteous women are the truly devout ones, who guard the intimacy which God has [ordained to be] guarded. As for those women whose ill-will you have reason to fear, admonish them [first]; then leave them alone in bed; then beat them; and if thereupon they pay you heed, don't seek to harm them. Behold, God is indeed most high, great"

Dr. Mohammad Mohsen Khan and
Dr. Mohammad Taqi-ud-din Al Hilali

The verse was also translated as follows in the *Interpretation of the Meaning of The Nobel Qur'an* in English Language: [20]

"Men are the protectors and maintainers of women, because Allah has made one of them excel the other, and because they spend (to support them) from their means. Therefore the righteous women are devoutly obedient (to Allah and their husbands) and guard in the husband's absence what Allah orders them to guard (e.g. her chastity, property, etc.). As to those women on whose part you see ill-conduct, admonish them (first), (next) refuse to share their beds, (and last) beat them (lightly if it is useful), but if they return to obedience, seek not against them means (of annoyance). Surely, Allah is Ever Most High, Most Great."

Similar translations can be found in Maulana Abdul Majid Daryabadi's commentary[21], in a new translation of the *Qur'an* by M. A. S. Abdel Haleem[22], in Dr. Ahmad Zidan's translation[23], *The Meaning of*

[20] Dr. Mohammad Mohsen Khan and Dr. Mohammad Taqi-ud-din Al Hilali, *Interpretation of the Meaning of The Nobel Qur'an* in English language, Part 1, first edition, 1989, Kazi Publications, Lahor, Pakistan

[21] Maulana Abdul Majid Dayrabadi, *Holy Qur'an with English Translation and Commentary,* Vol 1. The Taj Company Ltd., Karachi, Pakistan.

[22] M. A. S. Abdel Haleem, *The Qur'an, A New Translation.* Oxford University Press, Inc., New York, 2004.

[23] Dr. Ahmad Zidan, Mrs. Dina Zidan, *The Glorious Qur'an, Text and Transalation.* Islamic Home, publishing and Distribution, Cairo, Egypt.

The Glorious Qur'an [24], in a translation by Muhammad Pickthall, in the English version of Syyid Abul A'la Mawdudi's *Tafhim al-Qur'an* [25], in the translation and commentary of the *Qur'an* by Abdallah Yusuf Ali [26], in the translation and commentary [27] of T. B. Irving, in *The Fragile Vessels* [28], and finally in *The Nobel Qur'an, A New Rendering of its Meaning in English* [29], by Abdalhaqq and Aisha Bewley

In many of his lectures, Yusuf Estes [30] expresses his strong disagreement with any translation to the word *Udhdhribuuhon* in the verse as beat them or hit them. He supports his view by quoting the clear instructions of the Prophet Muhammad *SAAW* in his last sermon during the farewell pilgrimage, as well as numerous instructions given by the Prophet on other occasions. His support of this view is also based on the Prophet's own actions in this area. Yusuf is of the view that for any one to provide the proper translation of the word, one must be a scholar of both languages: the Arabic language and the language he is translating to. He also has to be a scholar of Islam to provide the proper translation.

The second meaning of the word *Udhdhribuuhon* is to distance yourself from them and can be found in the analysis of Dr. Abdulhamid

---

[24] Muhammad M. Pickthall, *The Meaning of The Glorious Qur'an, Text and Explanatory Translation*. Muslim World League, Mecca Al-Mukarramah, Saudi Arabia, 1977, p 80.

[25] Zafar Ishaq Ansari, *Towards Understanding the Qur'an*, Vol.II, Surah 4-6, English Version of *Tafhim al-Qur'an* by Syyid Abul A'la Mawdudi. The Islamic Foundation, Leicester, United Kingdom 1989, pp 35-36.

[26] Abdallah Yusuf Ali, *The Holy Qur'an, Translation and Commentary.* American Trust Publications for The Muslim Students' Association of the United States and Canada. 2nd Edition, June, 1977.

[27] T. B. Irving (Al-Hajj Ta'lim A'li), *The Qur'an, the Noble Reading, Translation and Commentary.* The Mother Mosque Foundation, Cedar Rapids, Iowa, USA, 1993.

[28] Muhammad Al-Jibaly *The Muslim Family-3 The Fragile Vessels*, Al-Kitaab and as Sunnah Publishing, Arlington Texas, 2000

[29] Abdalhaqq and Aisha Bewley, *The Nobel Qur'an, A New Rendering of its Meaning in English*. Bookwork, Norwich, 1999, printed at Dubai, U.A.E. p 73

[30] See http://www.islamtomorrow.com for many of Yusuf Estes' lectures on the subject. Here is a link for one example: www.youtubeislam.com/video/5534/What-is-Happening-with-Islam-and-Muslim-48

Abusulayman, as we will see in detail in the next chapter.[31] This is also the interpretation selected by Br. Yahiya Emerick in his new translation of the *Qur'an*, which, unfortunately, is not yet in print.

As for the third meaning, to have sexual intercourse with them, it is found in *Al-Qur'an, A Contemporary Translation*,[32] by Ahmed Ali. He provides the following translation:

"Men are the support of women as God gives some more means than others, and because they spend of their wealth (to provide for them). So women who are virtuous are obedient to God and guard the hidden as God guarded it. As for women you feel are averse, talk to them persuasively; then leave them alone in bed (without molesting them) and have intercourse with them, ie go to bed with them (when they are willing). If they open out to you, do not seek an excuse for blaming them. Surely God is Sublime and great."

In his response to a question related to Islam allowing men to beat their wives, Yusuf Estes provides the following translation:[33]

"Men are the protectors and maintainers of women, because Allah has made one of them to excel the other, and because they spend (to support them) from their means. Therefore the righteous women are devoutly obedient (to Allah), and guard in the husband's absence what Allah orders them to guard (e.g. their chastity, their husband's property, etc.). Regarding the woman who is guilty of lewd, or indecent behavior, admonish her (if she continues in this indecency then), stop sharing her bed (if she still continues doing this lewd behavior, then), [set forth for her the clear meaning of either straighten up or else we are finished and when she returns to proper behavior take up sharing the bed with her again], but if she returns in obedience (to proper behavior and conduct) then seek

---

[31] See reference 27

[32] Ahmed Ali, *Al Qur'an, A Contemporary Translation.* Princeton University Press, 41 William St., Princeton, New Jersey, fifth printing, 1994.

[33] See this link http://www.islamtomorrow.com/articles/women_treatment.htm

not against them means (of annoyance). Surely, Allah is Ever Most High, Most Great."

While this translation of the word *daraba* may seem strange, it is supported by Aby Alqasem Al-Husain Muhammad, known as Raghib Al-Asfahany, in his work **Al Mufradat fi Ghareeb Al-Qur'an.**[34] In this work, along with many other meanings of the word *Daraba* that he explained, he refers to *Daraba al Fahl Alnaqah*, which can be translated to "the he camel had intercourse with the she camel". As such, and as long as this meaning is available to us, and the language allows for this word to be used to describe such an act, we cannot ignore it in our analysis.

It is very clear that the above three interpretations are legitimate and possible for the word *Daraba*, and it is also very clear that none of them allow for the husband to strike his wife physically in any way that leads to physical pain or discomfort.

---

[34] Aby Alqasem Al-Husain Muhammad, known as Raghib Al-Asfahany, **Al Mufradat fi Ghareeb Al-Qur'an**. Dar Alma'refah lel- tebaa'h wal Nashr, Beirut, Lebanon

Interpretation of the *Qawamah* verse

INTRODUCTION

I n this section, we will present a highlight of the interpretation of verse 34 of *Surah Al-Nisa'* as it appears in various books of *Tafseer*. It is not our intention here to enlist all books of *Tafseer* and provide their detailed interpretation of the verse; we will only focus on some of the major books such as Ibn Katheer, Al-Fakhr Al-Razy, Al-Qrtoby, Al-Aloosy, **Mahasen Al-Ta'weel** from the earlier interpretation books and **Rawae'e Al Bayan, Fi-Zelal Al Qur'an, Tafheem ul Qur'an**, and **Al-Tafseer Al Muneer** and others from recent interpretation books. The purpose of quoting all these tafaseer books is to make sure we cover all points of discussion made by various scholars related to the verse at hand. As such, we will not present all the arguments discussed and examined in each and every one of these references. We will just talk about the unique points and ideas mentioned by each of the specific scholars to make sure that by the end of this section, we have collected almost all the ideas related to the interpretation of this verse. We will also put forward some of the comments emphasized by some of the contemporary scholars in their Qur'anic commentaries such as Sh. Muhammad Al-Ghazaly, Sh. Muhammad Metwally El-Sha'rawi, Ustaz Abdel Haleem Abu Shoqqah, Dr. Abdulhamid A. Abusulyman, Dr. Wahbah Al Zehaily, Dr. Jerald F. Dirks and Dr. Saalih ibn Ghaanim Al-Sadlaan.

Before quoting the specific and unique points of these scholars, let us start with a general interpretation of the verse covering the main points agreed upon by most of these references.

GENERAL INTERPRETATION OF THE VERSE [35]

In their interpretation of the verse of *Qawamah*, most of the Qur'anic interpreters (*mufassereen*) narrated on authority of al-Hasan al-Basri that the reason for the revelation of this verse was the following incident:

"A woman came to the Prophet *SAAW* complaining that her husband has slapped her on the face: the Prophet said: "retaliation." Then Allah revealed "Men are protectors and maintainers of women," so she didn't retaliate. In another narration, the Prophet said: We desired one thing but Allah wanted another, and that which Allah wants is best."[36]

In general, this verse speaks about four main ideas. These are:

1. Men are entrusted by Allah and given the responsibility to be the leaders of the family institution

2. The main two reasons Allah appointed men to be the leaders of the family institution are to do with the attributes He *SWT* endowed them with, as well as the responsibility of men to do their best to financially support and provide for the family

3. Women are divided into two camps with regards to the issue of men's leadership of the family. The first camp is represented by women who are righteous and obedient to Allah and to their husbands, as long as they don't ask or instruct their wives to do something contradicting Allah's order. The second camp is represented by rebellious and persistently disobedient women

4. A three stage approach should be followed in dealing with persistently disobedient and rebellious women

Various *Tafaseer* elaborate on each of the above four ideas and provide a variety of explanations supported by historical evidence from the biography of Prophet Muhammad *SAAW*, as well as from the practices of his companions to support their arguments, as we will see in the next few pages.

---

[35] Muhammad Ali Assabony, **Mukhtasar Tafseer Ibn Katheer**, Dar Al Qur'an Al Kareem, Beirut, Lebanon, 1402 H, 1981. Volume 1

[36] Ibn Jareer

Al-Fakhr Al-Razy

One of the very unique points that are highlighted by Imam Al-Fakhr Al-Razy is linking the verse to the previous verses in *Surah Al-Nisa'*.[37] The earlier verses in the Surah discussed the issue of inheritance and presented how it should be distributed among various survivors of the deceased. In most of the cases, men would end up receiving twice as much compared to women of the same relation to the deceased. Verse 34 is providing the main reason for such a distribution. It is not that Allah *SWT* is favouring one gender over the other, as some of those who like to attack Islam or those who don't understand it such as orientalists and feminist groups would have us believe. It is not that Islam considers women inferior to men. It is rather because Islam makes men responsible to take full care of their female relatives in particular and their families in general, and to provide them with the needed financial support among other forms of protection and support.

After putting forward the *Hadeeth* that was narrated by Omar ibn Al-Khattab *RAA*, related to allowing men to strike ladies, as indicated in the verse as the third step to deal with the *Nushooz*, another important point that he emphasizes is the view of Imam Al Shafeei *RAA* that it is **preferred not to use this permission** according to the above incident mentioned in the *hadeeth*. He called attention to the fact that the Prophet *SAAW* has said: **"Those are not the best of you"** (لا تجدون أولئك خياركم) , when he received the complaints of the ladies who were the victims of this kind of treatment from their husbands.

Al-Qortoby

In his *Al-Jame' Le-Ahkam Al-Qur'an*[38], Al-Qortoby emphasizes among other points, the following three very important points related to this verse:

---

[37] Mohammad Al-Razy Fakhr Al Deen, *Tafsee Al Fakhr Al Razy* Volume 9, Dar Al Fekr for printing, publishing and distribution, PP 90-93

[38] Aby Abdallah Muhammad ben Ahmad Al-Ansary al-Qortoby, *Al-Jame' Le-Ahkam Al-Qur'an* Arabic writer's House for printing and publications, Cairo, 1967, Volume 5 pp 168-174

• Scholars understood from the part of the verse that indicates that husbands should financially support their wives, that if a husband doesn't fulfill this condition he is not considered the leader of the family (*Qawwam*) any more and the wife, if she wishes would have the right to get out of the marriage contract.

• He indicates that *takhafoona noshozahona* (تخافون نشوزهن) means, according to Ibn Abbas *RAA*, that you are **certain** and **sure** without any doubt of their disobedience and defiant attitude.

• There is a defined period of time for the deserting of wives in bed. It could go from one month, as the Prophet *SAAW* did with Hafsah *RAA* when she told Aishah *RAA* the Prophet's secret[39], up to four months

Al-Aloosy

A key point we would like to highlight in this interpretation, is related to the linguistic approach used in the expression (بما فضل الله بعضهم على بعض) which means "Because of what God has given some persons advantages over others,". Allah *SWT* didn't say what could be translated as "Because of what God has given men advantages over women". This indicates that in general, men may have certain advantages (more equipped to carry on the responsibility of taking full care of the family), however, there are cases where certain women could be better than men in many areas.

Sheikh Muhammad Ali Assabony's comment

In his beautiful book ***Rawae'e Al-Bayan***[40], **Sh. Muhammad Ali Assabony** emphasized the same as indicated above in Al-Aloosy's *tafseer*. The fact that the expression used by Allah *SWT* (بما فضل الله بعضهم على بعض) which means "Because of what God has given some persons advantages over others" signifies two important points. These are:

---

[39] See the tafseer of *Surah At-Tahrim*, Q66
[40] Sheikh Muhammad Ali Assabony, ***Rawae'e Al-Bayan Tafseer Aayaat Al Ahkaam***, 'Vol One, Maktabat Al Ghazaly, Damascus, Syria, third print 1400 H, 1980, pp 466-467

• In general, the male gender may have certain advantages over the female gender (i.e. they may be more equipped to carry on the responsibility of taking full care of the family), however, this does not apply for all men and all women. In many cases, certain women could be better than men in specific areas.

• Men and women are parts of the same entity. They form the same body. Every organ of the human body is vital for the body to stay healthy and continue to function appropriately. Every organ has certain functions to perform. None of these organs is lesser in importance than the other, nor should it feel inferior compared to other organs.

Fi Zelal Al Qur'an

Syed Qutb, in his monumental work, **In the shade of the Qur'an (Fi Zelal Al Qur'an)** [41] emphasizes the following points related to this verse

• Family is the first and most important institution in human life in the sense that its influence is felt at each stage of human life

• The running and administration of a much inferior institution, such as those engaged in financial, political, and commercial affairs is normally assigned to those who are most qualified for the job by their education, training and natural ability

• Both man and woman are the creation of God, and He *SWT* does not wish to do injustice to anyone He created. Indeed He gives each of His creatures the abilities and talents that befit the job assigned to them

• Among the qualities the woman has been given are tenderness, quick reaction and an instinctive response to the needs of children, without the need for much deliberation and reflection. There is no external compulsion in this. It is an impulsive reaction, which the woman mostly enjoys despite the fact that it requires sacrifice from her. This is part of God's work, which is always perfect

---

[41] Sayyid Qutb, *In The Shade Of The Qur'an, Fi Zilal al Qur'an,* Translated and edited by Adil Salahi & Ashur Shamis, Volume 3, 2001/1421H, The Islamic Foundation

• These are not superficial qualities. Indeed, they are implanted in the woman's physical, mental, and psychological constitution. Some leading scientists believe that they are present in each cell in the woman's constitution, because they are rooted in the first cell that multiplies to form the foetus and the child

• Among the qualities a man is given are toughness, slow reaction and response, as well as proper thought and reflection before action. All his functions from the early days of being a hunter, gatherer, to fighting for the protection of his wife and children, to earning his living in any way, require some deliberation and consideration before taking a decision and implementing it. These qualities are also deeply rooted in man's constitution

• Man's qualities make him more able and better equipped to take charge of the family. Similarly, his duty to support his family, as part of that general distribution of functions, makes him more suited to overall authority

• The **Qur'an** states that in Islamic society men are required to look after women. It is an assignment of duties on the basis of natural abilities and the fair distribution of responsibilities. Each party is assigned the duties most suited to its nature

• Men assuming the status of family leadership or guardianship (*Qawamah*) **does not by any means lead to the negation of the women's character and role in the family home and in society at large. Nor does it mean the cancellation of her civil status**

• Devotion means willing obedience, motivated by love, not the sort of obedience enforced against one's will

• The ones who are not righteous are described here as rebellious. Their rebellion is given a physical description derived from standing on a high position to declare their mutiny. Islam does not wait for such a rebellion to take place, nor for the roles to become so confused that the family institution splits into two camps. When the situation reaches that point, it is almost impossible to sort out. At this point, gradual treatment must be administered in order to preserve the family and protect it from destruction. The one who is in charge is allowed to take some disciplinary measures that are often effective. He does not take them as retaliatory measures or to humiliate or to torture his partner, but to achieve reconciliation and preserve the family in the very early stage of dispute.

• **Needless to say that there is no question of any of these measures being resorted to in the case of a healthy relationship between a man and his wife.** Again, they are preventative measures taken in an unhealthy situation to protect the family against collapse

• **The procedure described in the verse is by no means applicable to all women.** However, those types of women do exist who should be treated this way, and Islam considers this measure a last resort used necessarily to safeguard the family.

• At the same time, the measures included in the verse are accompanied by a stern warning against misuse

• The above measures also should not be used if it is felt that they will be ineffective or even counterproductive. In such situations Islam recommends a different process as described in the next verse of the same *surah* [42]

Mahasen Al Ta'weel

The scholar Muhammad Jamal Aldeen Al-Qasemy, in his tafseer, **Mahasen Al-Ta'weel** [43], among other points, stresses the following important thesis referring to Imam Al Seiooty in *al Ekleel*:

"Since one of the *Qawamah* conditions and requirements according to the verse is the responsibility of men to spend from their own money to provide the family needs, if a husband can't fulfill this condition, he is not *Qawwam* any more. He has no right neither to be the head of the family, nor to prevent his wife from going outside home to seek employment in any honourable manner."

---

[42] (Q4, V35)
[43] Muhammad Jamal Al-Qasemy, *Tafseer Al-Qasemy, Mahasen Al-Ta'weel* Chapter 5 Dar Ihyaa' Al-Kutob Al-A'rabiah, Cairo, Egypt

Tafheem ul Qur'an

Sayyid Abul A'la Mawdudi in his **Tafheem al-Qur'an commentary**[44] emphasizes the following points:

- A *qawwam* or *qayyam* is a person responsible for administering and supervising the affairs of either an individual or an organization, for protecting and safeguarding them and taking care of their needs
- The verb used to indicate that one of the sexes was endowed with certain qualities which Allah has not endowed the other sex with, does not mean that some people have been invested with superior honour and dignity.
- The qualities given to the male qualifies him to function as the head of the family
- The female has been so constituted that she should live under the male care and protection
- It should be borne in mind that obedience to God has priority over a woman's duty to obey her husband. If a woman's husband either asks her to disobey God or prevents her from performing a duty imposed on her by God, she should refuse to carry out her husband's command.
- The three stages to resolve marital discord described in the verse should not be resorted to by a man all at once, but they may only be **employed if a wife adopts an attitude of obstinate defiance.**

A. Yusuf Ali *Commentary*

The following are some of A. Yusuf Ali's comments on the *Qawamah* verse:

- *Qawwam* means one who stands firm in another's business, protects his interest, and looks after his affairs, it also means standing firm in his own business, and managing affairs with a steady purpose
- The good wife is obedient and harmonious in her husband's presence, and in his absence guards his reputation and property and her own virtue, as ordained by God

---

[44] See reference No. 15

• In case of family jars, four steps are mentioned, to be taken in that order: (1) perhaps verbal advice or admonition may be sufficient; (2) if not, sex relations may be suspended; (3) if this is not sufficient, some slight physical correction may be administered; **but Imam Shafi'i considers this inadvisable**, though permissible, and all authorities are unanimous in deprecating any sort of cruelty, even of the nagging kind; (4) if all these fail, a family council is recommended

Al-Tafseer Al-Muneer

In his wonderful *tafseer; Al-Tafseer Al-Muneer*, Dr. Wahbah Al-Zehaily, lays emphasis on the following points related to this verse[45]:

• Family leadership and guidance (*Qawamah*) should never be understood to mean dictatorship and stubbornness on men's part when they deal with their wives.

• **Before following the three step solution suggested in the verse, there has to be clear evidence and proof without a doubt that the wife is committing *nushooz*, persisting in disobeying her husband, and not fulfilling her duties as a wife.**

• Aside from the *Qawamah* status, men and women have equal rights according to the *Qur'an*[46].

• Women have their own independent financial freedom and are neither required nor can be forced by any one to spend out of their own money to support the family. They only do this if they choose to out of their own kindness and love to help their families.

• *Qawamah* status is a burden that is suitable for the abilities and potentials that Allah SWT has bestowed on men and men should honour it and carry out their responsibility in the best possible way

• **Although symbolic beating which does not cause harm or leave bruises is permitted, the majority of scholars have agreed that it is preferred not to practice it.**

---

[45] Dr. Wahbah Al-Zaihaily, *Al-Tafseer Al-Muneer fi Alaqeedah wal-Sharee'ah wal Manhaj*, Volume 5, Dar Al-Fekr, Damascus, Syria, PP 52-57
[46] (Q2, V228)

Sh. Muhammad Al-Ghazaly's Commentary

In his valuable book, *A Thematic Commentary on The Qur'an*[47] Sh. Muhammad Al-Ghazaly states in his comment on this verse "A pertinent question arises here: what is to be done when it is the woman who persecutes the husband or treats him with insolence? The family home is certain to turn into hell. Under these **exceptional circumstances**, Islam prescribes a gradual solution that allows, as a first step, for simple advice and gentle persuasion, followed by a temporary cessation of sexual contact, and then and only then, permits resort to physical measures. The main condition attached to this last method is that physical punishment must be moderate and should not in any way touch the face or harm it. Looking closely into the *Sunnah* of the Prophet *SAAW*, however, **I cannot find a justification for this last measure except when the wife refuses vehemently and persistently to engage in the intimate relation with the husband or brings male outsiders into their home in the absence of her husband. Both of which represent, as we can see, very serious problems indeed.**"[48]

Sh. Muhammad Metwally Al-Sha'rawy Commentary

In his commentary of the Qur'an, Sh. Muhammad Metwally Al-Sha'rawy[49] emphasized the following points about verse 34 of *Surah Al Nisaa'*:

• This verse talks about men and women in general, not particularly about husbands and wives only. It covers fathers and mothers, brothers and sisters, etc. As such it is the responsibility of males in the family to

---

[47] Sh. Muhammad Al-Ghazaly, *A Thematic Commentary on The Qur'an,* Volume I, page 63, Translated by Ashur A. Shamis, International Institute of Islamic Thought, Herndon, Virginia, USA, 1420AH/1999AC

[48] Author modified the translation based on the understanding of the original Arabic text of Sh. Muhammad Al-Ghazaly's work available in **Nahwa Tafseer Madooe'y Lesewar Al-Qur'an Al-Kareem**, page 50, seventh edition, Dar Al-Shrooq, Cairo, Egypt

[49] **Sh. Muhammad Metwaly Al-Sha'rawy Comments on Qur'an,** *Vol 28, Dar Akhbar Al Yoom,,* Cairo, Egypt Vol 28

take good care of their female relatives and strive hard to provide for them a dignified life

• The concept of *Qawamah* puts women in general in a very distinguished and noble state and requires from men to consistently work hard and do their best to ensure the finest and most excellent provision and life style for those women whom they are taking care of and they are responsible for

• The use of the word *Qawwamon* (emphasis expression) indicates that Allah *SWT* is entrusting men with an enormous and great responsibility to be fulfilled according to this verse. For men to accomplish this task they have to work tirelessly and diligently to discharge this responsibility

• Working tirelessly and striving hard to provide a dignified life for the family is the number one duty of men. Women shouldn't be forced to go out to earn a living and support the family. The **Qur'an** makes this very clear in the story of Adam and Satan[50]

• Allah endowed most men with certain qualities to equip them to carry out their responsibilities as *Qawwamon*. At the same time, Allah *SWT* gifted most women with other qualities and capabilities (not necessarily the same as those He gave to men) to be able to provide peace and tranquility in their family life and help men carry out their family obligations. This, in no way means that one gender is superior over the other and the other is inferior. It means that both genders complement each other to ensure the most successful, positive, and healthy family life for all family members. That is why the verse said (بما فضل الله بعضهم على بعض) which means "Because of what God has given some persons advantages over others,". Allah *SWT* didn't say what could be translated as "Because of what God has given men advantages over women."

• Most men fail to select the right time for giving advice (فعظوهن).They usually try to advise their women during the conflict and when they are at odds with each other. This is not the right time. For the advice to be

---

[50] (Q20, V117)

effective, it has to be done at the suitable time when both are close to each other, at cherished moments of warmness and nearness

• Most men also fail to use the proper language and a gentle approach when they advise their women. For the advice to be effective, men should present it in a tender and moderate way and ought to avoid being rough.

• "Deserting them in bed" can only be done after the failure of advice given in the proper way. Deserting them has to be done in bed. Don't desert them and sleep in another room in the house. Other family members who live in the same house shouldn't know that there is a problem between the husband and the wife. This provides a better chance for the problem to be solved. As such, the husband should stay in the same room with the wife and also sleep in the same bed, but not engage her in any intimate physical relations.

• Only when all the above measures fail to bring a resolution to the problem can the husband resort to light beating to indicate his displeasure with the situation. The beating has to be very light using something like a *Miswak* (tooth brush).

Mohamed Asad's Commentary

The following footnote appeared in Mohamed Asad's commentary on the Nobel *Qur'an* [51]. It provides his views and explains some of the terminologies used in the verse:

• The expression *qawwam* is an intensive form of *qai'm* ("one who is responsible for" or "takes care of" a thing or a person). Thus *qama a'la'l-mar'ah* signifies "he undertook the maintenance of the women" or "he maintained her". The grammatical form of *qawwam* is more comprehensive than *qa'im*, and combines the concepts of physical maintenance and protection as well as of moral responsibility: and it is because of the last-named factor that I have rendered this phrase as "men shall take full care of women".

---

[51] Mohammad Asad, *The Message of the Qur'an* Translated and Explained, Dar Al-Andalus, Gibraltar

• The term *nushuz* ("rebellion"- here rendered an "ill-will") comprises every act of deliberate bad behaviour of a wife towards her husband or of a husband towards his wife, including what is nowadays described as "mental cruelty"; with reference to the husband, it also denotes "ill treatment", in the physical sense, of his wife (cf. verse 128 of the same *surah*). In this context, a wife's "ill-will" implies a deliberate, persistent breach of her marital obligations.

• It is evident from many authentic Traditions that the Prophet *SAAW* himself intensely detested the idea of beating one's wife, and said on more than one occasion, "Could any of you beat his wife as he would beat a slave, and then lie with her in the evening?" (*Bukhari* and *Muslim*). According to another Tradition, he **forbade the beating of any women** with the words, "Never beat God's handmaidens" (Abu Dawood, Nasa'i, Ibn Majah, Ahmad Ibn Hanbal, Ibn Hebban, and Hakim, on the authority of Iyas ibn Abd Allah; Ibn Hebban on the authority of 'Abd Allah ibn 'Abbas; and Bayhaqi on the authority of Umm Kulthoom). When the above verse authorizing the beating of a refractory wife was revealed, the Prophet is reported to have said: "I wanted one thing but God has willed another thing and what God has willed must be best" (see *Manar* V, 74). With all this, he stipulated in his sermon on the occasion of the Farewell Pilgrimage, shortly before his death, that beating should be resorted to only if the wife **"has become guilty, in an obvious manner, of immoral conduct"**, and that it should be done "in such a way as not to cause pain (*ghayr mubarrih*)"; authentic Traditions to this effect are found in Muslim, Tirmidhi, Abu Dawood, Nasa'i, and Ibn Majah. On the basis of these traditions, all the authorities stress that this "beating", if resorted to at all, should be more or less symbolic- "with a toothbrush, or some such thing" (Tabri quoting the views of scholars of the earliest times), or even "with a folded handkerchief" (Razi); and some of the greatest Muslim scholars (e.g. Ash-Shafi'i) are of the opinion that it is just barely permissible, and should preferably be avoided: and they justify this opinion by the Prophet's personal feelings with regard to this problem.

The Fragile Vessels

Muhammad al-Jibaly in the third book of his series on *The Muslim Family; The Fragile Vessels* [52] emphasizes the following points:

• A leader will inevitably have to deal with the "dirty" job of discipline. Discipline is an important process that must be properly implemented. It has its rules and regulations. Violating those rules would undermine or invalidate the whole process, and may bring about more damage than good.

• Ibn Kathir commented on the words, "Exalted and Great" at the end of the *Qawamah* verse saying: "This carries a strong warning to the men when they transgress over the women without a reason. Indeed, Allah, the Exalted and Great, is then the women's protector, and He will surely take revenge against anyone who oppresses them or transgresses over them"

• One may ask, "What is the benefit of light hitting?" The answer is that a women normally has a sensitive nature; the slightest show of discourtesy to her would tremendously affect her and cause her to rethink her actions. If, on the other hand, light hitting does not work with her, brutal hitting won't

• We should keep in mind that the purpose of hitting is to correct and remind, and not to revenge or harm

• Even though a man is allowed to hit his wife in certain extreme situations, hitting her is disliked by Islam and is considered the resort of the helpless

• Many husbands are abusive to their wives, justifying their action by the texts that command the wife to obey the husband or allow him to discipline her. Those husbands must understand that discipline is a well-regulated matter in Islam, and has no room for abuse. An abusive husband is indeed an oppressor and an abused wife has the full right to turn to justice and seek punishment of her abusive husband

Ahmed Ali's Comment

In his comments on the verse, Ahmed Ali [53] emphasizes that *Qawwam*

---

[52] Muhammad Al-Jibaly *The Muslim Family-3 The Fragile Vessels,* Al-Kitaab and as Sunnah Publishing, Arlington Texas, 2000
[53] Ahmed Ali, *Al Qur'an, A Contemporary Translation*, Princeton University Press, 41 William St. Princeton, New Jersey, fifth printing, 1994

does not mean lord or master, but provider of food and necessities of life, and through this provisioning becomes the *qaim*, or the caregiver. He also indicates that apart from the meaning of "*Nushuz*" as rising up or ill treatment, it also means aversion to an act. He also translates the word *daraba* as to go to bed with them based on the meaning given by Raghib in *Al-Mufradat fi Gharib Al-Qur'an*, and points out that it can't be taken as "to strike them" as this contradicts the clear practice of Prophet Muhammad *SAAW* as well as his advice in authentic *hadeeth* reported by Al Bukhary and Muslim, such as, "Could any of you beat your wife as he would a slave, and then lie with her in the evening?" He also indicates that there are other traditions in Abu Da'ud , Nasa'i, Ibn Majah, Ahmad bin Hanbal and others, to the effect that he forbade the beating of women, saying: "Never beat God's handmaidens."

Dr. Abdulhamid Abusulayman

In his valuable work, *"Marital Discord, Recapturing the Islamic Spirit of Human Dignity"*[54] Dr. Abdulhamid Abusulayman discusses the use of the word (*daraba*) and its derivatives in Qur'an and finds that it has many meanings, possibly reaching up to seventeen distinct nuances other than just slapping, striking, or beating. Here are some of these meanings:

• "God **propounds** (to you) the parable...."[55]

• "When Jesus the son of Mary is **held up as an example**, behold, your people raise a clamor threat (in ridicule)!"[56]

• "See what **similes they strike** for thee: but they have gone astray, and never can they find a way"[57]

• "When you **travel through** the earth...."[58]

• "Then we **covered** their ears for a number of years, in the Cave"[59]

---

[54] Dr. Abdulhamid A. Abusulayman, *Marital Discord, Recapturing the Islamic Spirit of Human Dignity*, The International Institute of Islamic Thought, 2003, Herndon, VA, USA

[55] (Q16, V75, V76, V112 and Q66, V11)

[56] (Q43, V57)

[57] (Q17, V48)

[58] (Q4, V101)

[59] (Q18, V11)

- "Shall We then **take away** the Revelation from you and repel [you], because you are a people transgressing beyond bounds"[60]
- "….they should **draw their veils** over their bosoms…..and that they should not **strike their feet** so as to draw attention to their hidden ornaments…."[61]
- "Then We told Moses: **Strike the sea with your staff.** So it divided and each separate part resemble the huge firm mass of mountain"[62]
- "God does not disdain to **use the similitude** of things, lowest as well as highest….."[63]
- "O you who attain to faith! When you **go abroad** in the cause of God, investigate carefully…."[64]
- "…So a wall **shall be erected** between them, with a gate therein. Within it will be mercy throughout, and outside it, all alongside, will be [wrath] and punishment!"[65]

Dr. Abusulayman concludes that the verb *daraba* has many meanings depending on the context of the use. These meanings cover a huge spectrum. They can range from *travel* or *depart* when the word is used with land, to *block* or *prevent* when it is used with ears, and can also mean to *distinguish*, to *draw*, to *strike a path*, to *partition and separate*, to be *overshadowed*, to *cut, slash, strike*, to *impel, shock*, or to *damage*, all depending on the context.

In his view, and considering the Islamic spirit of spousal relations and the practice of Prophet Muhammad *SAAW* in this regard, he thinks that the word *daraba* in the verse means that husbands should distance themselves from their wives if admonishing them and refusing to share their beds doesn't bring the required resolution of marital problems and the restoration of love and harmony between estranged spouses. He thinks that leaving the marital home and moving away or separating from the

---

[60] (Q43, V5)
[61] (Q24, V31)
[62] (Q26, V63)
[63] (Q2, V26)
[64] (Q4, V94)
[65] (Q75, V13)

wife would be the last resort before seeking the mediation of arbiters from their respective families.

Ustaz Abdel Haleem Abu Shoqah

In his monumental work *Tahreer Al-Mara'h Fi Asr Al-resalah*,[66] Ustaz Abdle Haleem Abu Shoqah emphasizes the following points related to spousal relations in Islam:

• The main framework of fulfilling spousal obligations between husband and wife is that of *Mawadah* (positive and healthy love) and *Rahmah* (mercy and kindness). If the warmth of *Mawadah* declines for any reasons, the rights are preserved because of the *Rahmah* between the spouses.

• There are many mutual obligations that both spouses should observe and try to fulfill towards each other such as:

   – Kindness

   – Mercy

   – The desire to have children

   – Trust

   – Sharing in easy and difficult times

   – Being neat and clean

   – Fulfilling each others' sexual needs

   – Entertaining

   – Positive Jealousy

   – Mutual respect, particularly during the process of separation

• Family leadership (*Qawamah*) is a religious duty and responsibility that Allah entrusted the husband with. He, the husband must strive hard to fulfill this duty in the best possible way

• Some scholars see the extra degree that Allah has given to men as the verse (وللرجال عليهن درجة)[67] indicates, in addition to their responsibility in leading the family, to mean that men have to be more forgiving towards

---

[66] Abdel Haleem Abu Shoqah, *Tahreer Al-Mara'h Fi Asr Al Resalah,* Volume 5, The place of women in the family. Dar Al Qalam for publications and Distribution, Kwait,

[67] (Q2, V228)

women and have to overlook some of their wives' minor mistakes in the spousal relationship

• *Shura* (consulting) is a religious right for every Muslim. It has to be practiced in every sphere of life. *Shura* in family life is an obligation on the husband. He has to consult with family members before making decisions with respect to family matters.

• The husband/wife relationship is very private and much deeper than any other relationship. As such, the **Qur'an** tries to reduce others' intervention in it to the minimum, and only when it reaches a very critical situation. These critical situations could be either the misuse of the husband's authority, or the obstinate persistent disobedience of the wife to her husband

• Family leadership (*Qawamah*) can't be fulfilled without cooperation between husband and wife in the following three areas:

– Voluntary obedience of the wife to her husband in areas that don't contradict Allah's orders

– Mutual consultations between husband and wife in all areas related to family life

– The wife's fulfillment of her responsibility to take care of the family during her husband's absence

• Islam describes many ways to resolve marital conflicts, starting with many preventative measures and ending with separation and divorce. In between, there are many methods to be exhausted, in order, before resorting to the next one

• Beating, slapping or striking (*Darb*), should only be used in very specific cases where the mistake committed by the wife could have reached the stage of obscenity (*fahishah*), harming the husband's honor, such as allowing other men to enter his house without his permission

• The rules and laws described by Islam are for all times and all places. They are also for all of the various personalities created by Allah *SWT*. One method used as one step in the process of resolving marital conflict could be suitable for certain women in certain environments but not suitable for others. **The recommendation of Prophet Muhammad *SAAW* is not to use this approach with any women, even those who are not educated or at a very low degree intellectually when compared to their husbands. As such, in an environment where women are as educated as men and most of them are at the same intellectual level, *darb* should not be used**

• In addition to the text recommending *darb* as one of the stages to resolve marital conflict **there are many texts that recommend avoiding the use of this method**

• Even when it is used as the last resort in a very specific situation, there are many strict guidelines that accompany this method to make sure it does not negatively affect the spousal relationship, such as the following:

– It is purely symbolic and must be very gentle, to the extent that some scholars recommended the use of something similar to a toothbrush (*Miswak*)

– The face has to be completely avoided

– It should not be accompanied by yelling, shouting, or any form of verbal humiliation

Dr. Saalih ibn Ghaanim Al-Sadlaan

In his work, **Marital Discord (al-Nushooz)**,[68] Dr. Saalih ibn Ghaanim Al-Sadlaan, discusses the *Nushooz*, its definition, cases, causes, means of protection from it, and its remedy from **Qur'an** and *Sunnah*. In his analysis he talks about *Nushooz* from both the wife's side as well as from the husband's side. Here are some important points that have been highlighted in his work and which could be of benefit to our research:

• According to **Qur'an**, *Nushooz*, does not only happen from the wife towards the husband, it also occurs from the husband towards the wife. The **Qur'an** describes the proper solution for both cases[69]

• *Nushooz*, as summarized from the four recognized schools of thought

---

[68] Dr. Saalih ibn Ghaanim Al-Sadlaan, **Marital Discord (al-Nushooz)**. Al-Basheer publications and Translations, Translated by Jamaal al-Din M. Zarabozo, 1996

[69] (Q4, V34, V128)

(Hanafi, Maliki, Shafi'i, and Hanbali), could be from both spouses, regardless of whether it is due to disobedience, hatred, contrariness, diffidence, harshness, aggression, or harm by one of them

• The three-step remedy (1. admonition and guidance, 2. Boycotting, 3. [Disciplinary] beating) of the wife's *nushooz* explained in the *Qawamah* verse is only applied when it is made very clear that the *nushooz* is because of her behaviour, as she has become unruly and is committing sin and transgression

• The length of boycotting (step 2) is agreed upon by scholars and jurists as follows:

– Boycotting with respect to talking to her, this act must not be in excess of three days

– As for boycotting the bed, the husband can do this for as long as he believes that it will lead to her stopping her acts of *nushooz*. However, scholars have stated the furthest limit of such avoidance to be four months as that is the furthest limit of *al-eela* [70]

Dr. Jerald F Dirks Commentary

In his significant work **The Abrahamic Faiths,** [71] Dr. J. F. Dirks, after a clear and detailed discussion on how Islam liberated women, points out the following with regards to this verse:

"Despite the above information regarding the status of the wife in a Muslim marriage, some Western commentators on Islam have seized on part of one verse of the **Qur'an** to insist that Islam permits husbands to beat their wives. The relevant verse is as follows.

"As to those women on whose part ye fear disloyalty and ill-conduct, admonish them (first), (next), refuse to share their beds, (and lastly) beat them (lightly); but if they return to obedience, seek not against them means (of annoyance): for God is most high, great (above you all). (**Qur'an** 4:34b)

[70] This is where a husband takes an oath not to approach his wife. It is discussed in **Qur'an** in Surah al-Baqara verse 226

[71] See reference 61

"The Arabic word that is translated as "beat" in the above verse is "Udhdhribuu," which literally means to strike. The English word "beat" is an unfortunate translation, as it conveys the erroneous impression of a beating being administered. In contrast, "strike" covers the whole range of possibilities from a slight tap to a forceful punch, and it is only upon turning to the sayings of Prophet Muhammad that a proper understanding of the above Qur'anic verse can be achieved.

"There are numerous sayings of Prophet Muhammad that are relevant to a correct understanding of the above Qur'anic verse. Summing across these narrations, which are quoted below, one quickly discovers that husbands are not allowed to "strike" their wives except in the case "of flagrant misbehavior," and even then they may not "inflict upon them any severe punishment." Furthermore, a husband is enjoined that he may "not strike her on the face" etc.

"'Amr ibn Al-Ahwas Al-Jushami narrated that he heard the Prophet say in his farewell address on the eve of his Last Pilgrimage, after he had glorified and praised God, he cautioned his followers: "Listen! Treat women kindly…Should they be guilty of flagrant misbehavior, you may remove them from your beds and beat them, but do not inflict upon them any severe punishment…" (**Al-Tirmidhi,** Hadith #276)

"Hakim ibn Mu'awiyah Al-Qushairi quoted his father as saying that he asked the Apostle of God, "What is the right of the wife of one of us over him?" He replied: "That you should give her food when you eat, clothe her when you clothe yourself, do not strike her on the face, do not revile her or separate yourself from her except in the house." (**Abu Dawud,** Hadith #2137)

"Mu'awiyah Al-Qushairi said: "I went to the Apostle of God and asked him: 'What do you say about our wives?' He replied: 'Give them food what you have for yourself, and clothe them by which you clothe yourself, and do not beat them, and do not revile them.'" (**Abu Dawud,** Hadith #2139; see also Abu Dawud, Hadith #2138)

"'Abd Allah ibn Zama narrated that the Prophet forbade laughing at a person who passes wind and said, "How does anyone of you beat his wife as he beats the stallion camel, and then he may embrace (sleep with) her?" (**Al-Bukhari,** *Hadith* #8:68)

"…The Messenger of God…addressed the people, saying…"Fear God concerning women! Verily you have taken them on the security of God, and intercourse with them has been made lawful unto you by words of God. You too have right over them, and that they should not allow anyone to sit on your bed whom you do not like. But if they do that, you can chastise them, but not severely…" (**Muslim,** *Hadith* #2803)

"The sum total of the above narrations illustrates that **Qur'an** 4:34b does not allow a husband to "beat" his wife in any way that causes injury or physical harm. In short, the "beating" referred to in **Qur'an** 4:34b is akin to a private psychodrama in which the husband symbolically expresses his displeasure, and it is similar to the American idiom of "being beaten with a wet noodle." Just as Shakespeare's Merchant of Venice could have his pound of flesh only if he did not spill a single drop of blood, so can the husband "beat" his wife only if he does not cause any physical pain, harm, or injury. So much for the erroneous and slanderous statements that Islam allows husbands to beat their wives."

Proper Understanding of the *Qawamah* Concept

QAWAMAH, IMPORTANT CONCEPT TO BE UNDERSTOOD

We feel that proper understanding of the concept of *Qawamah* is a very important shared obligation of both spouses as we have indicated in our book, **Blissful Marriage**.[72] There are a great many Muslim spouses who don't understand the concept of *Qawamah* in Islam. Most spouses go to one extreme or the other in misunderstanding this concept. One extreme is represented in men who think that the meaning of *Qawamah* is to boss their wives around and to order them to do whatever they want whenever they wish while the wives have no choice but to obey and accept the husbands' views on everything. The other extreme is represented by ladies who blindly follow the feminist movement and don't want to recognize that their husbands have a certain status and responsibility given to them by Allah *SWT* to provide family protection and maintenance. This group refuses to recognize that there are natural differences between males and females and want to go against the rights and responsibilities given by Allah to men via this status of *Qawamah*. Both of these positions are extremes and are not accepted by Islam. We feel that it is of utmost importance that both spouses understand properly what *Qawamah* means, its privileges, its responsibilities, how it affects marital life and the consequences of not assuming it by husbands or refusing it by wives. *Qawamah* simply could be summarized as maintenance and protection, as indicated by Dr. Badawi in his valuable booklet, *The Status of Women in Islam*[73]. He writes, "The rules of married life in Islam are clear and in harmony with upright human

---

[72] Drs. Ekram and Mohamed Rida Beshir, **Blissful Marriage: A Practical Islamic Guide,** amana publications, Beltsville, MD, second edition 2005, pp 168-170

[73] Dr. Jamal Badawi, **Status of Women in Islam**, American Trust Publication, Indianapolis, Indiana, February 1983

nature. In consideration of the physiological and psychological make up of men and women, both have equal rights and claims on one another, except for one responsibility, that of leadership. This is a matter which is natural in any collective life and which is consistent with the nature of man. The **Qur'an** thus states,

> 'And they (women) have rights similar to those (of men) over them, and men are a degree above them'[74]

This degree is *Qawamah* (maintenance and protection). This refers to that natural difference between the sexes, which entitles the physically weaker sex to protection. It implies no superiority or advantage before the law. Yet a man's role of leadership in relation to his family does not mean that a husband is a dictator over his wife. Islam emphasizes the importance of taking counsel and mutual agreement in family decisions. The **Qur'an** gives us an example:

> '..If they (husband and wife) desire to wean the child by mutual consent and after consultation, there is no blame on them...'[75]

It is to be emphasized that this is just a division of labor and role differentiation. It does not, in any way, mean any categorical discrimination or superiority of one sex to the other.

Although this degree of *Qawamah* gives the man the authority to make the final decision in matters related to family, it also entrusts him with the responsibility to consult with his wife and to provide protection and maintenance to the family in the best way possible.

It is important here to point out that some husbands abuse this privilege, and, in the name of obedience, mistreat their wives with requests that are at the very least unreasonable. They constantly boss them around and order them to do things, and if their wives say they're tired, or that they can't keep up, their husbands complain that their wives are not

---

[74] (Q2, V228)

[75] (Q2, V233)

obeying them. Some of them may even say, "You have to obey me; otherwise you won't go to paradise". For example, a husband may be watching his favorite TV program after dinner, while the wife may be busy cleaning the kitchen and preparing the milk formula for her baby who is crying. Rather than preparing a cup of tea for himself, the husband orders his wife to make it for him. If she says, "I'm busy preparing the formula for the baby," he may consider this an act of disobedience from her. This is clearly unfair. This is not what is meant by obedience. A wife is not a slave. The husband has to be considerate and sensitive to the wife's condition and situation. Another example is when a husband, after dinner, asks his wife to go with him to visit a member of his family or a close relative. The wife may be exhausted from a long day of work and attending to their children. She may respond by saying, "can we do this on another evening?" Rather than being considerate and understanding her reasons for this, some husbands may consider this as an act of disobedience on their wives part.

In the next two chapters, we will provide the reader with many stories illustrating the appropriate use of *Qawamah*, as well as the inappropriate use. Our aim is to try to exhaust as many cases as we can to make sure the concept is clearly and properly understood by both husband and wife alike. This will no doubt go a long way in helping to ensure that the cornerstone of the Muslim society, the Muslim family, is a very strong and healthy institution that can provide a positive environment for the new Muslim generation to grow into strong and confident citizens, benefiting themselves and their families, and contributing to the wellbeing of their society as well as humanity at large.

QAWAMAH, A RESPONSIBILITY AND OBLIGATION TO BE FULFILLED

It is clear from the analysis presented in this book, based on the study of the meaning of the word *Qawamah* in authentic Arabic dictionaries as well as other dictionaries, the use of the word in the **Qur'an** and the explanations of many scholars and Qur'anic interpreters (*Mufassereen*), that

Qawama is an enormous responsibility entrusted by Allah on men. It is the responsibility to lead the Muslim family, take charge of its affairs, and provide guidance, maintenance, and sustenance for the family members. It is a colossal duty to protect and safeguard the family. It is a massive obligation on the husband's part to help and assist family members in satisfying their needs and achieving their noble goals in life. This enormous commitment can't be fulfilled without cooperation, consultation, and counselling with the wife, as well as with the rest of family members if they are at the age of maturity. The head of the family will bring wonderful goodness to the various relationships within the family when he practices *Qawamah* properly and fulfills its duties and requirements.

According to Esam Ben Muhammad al Shareef[76] for *Qawamah* to be fulfilled, it requires both husband and wife to posses the following three components:

- ***Taqwa of Allah SWT.*** This fear of God and being conscience of their duties towards Allah will guarantee that both husband and wife are observing the rights of each other and fulfilling the duties towards each other. This relationship based on *Mawadah* and *Rahmah* will ensure a positive and healthy family atmosphere. With *taqwa*, the husband wouldn't act as a dictator and there would be no place for selfishness or greed in marital life. With this, administering the home and exercising the duties of *qawamah* would be done in a calm, positive and proper way from the husband's side and with cooperation, trust, and acceptance from the wife

- **Proper understanding of the real meaning of *Qawamah*.** This knowledge will protect both husband and wife from any deviations during the practical implementation of *qawamah* in their family life. Also, the realization of the right meaning of *qawamah* requires that the husband, particularly, should learn from Prophet Muhammad *SAAW's* life and the way he conducted himself as a husband. He should understand deeply and

---

[76] Essam Ben Muhammad al Shareef, **Who has the Qawamah at home**, Said Al-Fawaed Al-Islamiah online library, pp55-57

know how he perfectly applied the concept of *qawamah* in his house, not only with one wife, but with more than one, while he was carrying the heaviest responsibility ever carried by a human. Prophet Muhammad *SAAW* is our model and example, and we are supposed to learn from his conduct and emulate him in every aspect of our life, and *qawamah* is no different

• **Good manners.** This will ensure that the husband is kind and that he deals with his wife gently. He will exercise patience and overlook many of the wife's shortcomings. As a result of this leniency in dealing, the wife will also respond in a positive and agreeable way to her husband's requests in various areas of interactions in their family life. This will certainly contribute to a long-lasting and healthy marital relationship, and ensure the formation of a very strong family. Both husband and wife will live happily hoping that in the Hereafter they will be in the company of the Prophet *SAAW* since he said, "The closest of you to me on the day of judgment are those who have good manners" [77]

QAWAMAH AND DOMESTIC VIOLENCE

There is no doubt that Islam liberated women and contributed positively towards the restoration of women's dignity and rights. Any fair-minded people who study the original sources of Islam, i.e. the **Qur'an** and the teachings of Prophet Muhammad *SAAW* would undoubtedly, easily reach this obvious and clear conclusion. However, many cultural practices of some Muslims from different ethnic backgrounds are completely contrary to Islam's teachings regarding women. These practices have certainly contributed in a negative way to the status of women in Islam. Islam holds women in very high and noble position as a mother, as a wife, as a sister, as a daughter, as an aunt, and as a grandmother. Needless to say that if we compare the situation of women before the advent of Islam in various corners of the globe, including the Arabian Peninsula

---

[77] *Saheeh al Jame' al Sagheer*

itself, with what Islam did for women; we can see the huge difference in women's status and rights in favour of Islam.

However, this is not the image and impression that non Muslims have about Islam and Muslim women. In fact, it is not even the understanding among many Muslims, due to so many cultural distortions. Realizing this, in the recent century particularly, many scholars have elaborated in various works on the true status of women in Islam, in many languages. Among these works are, **Status of Women in Islam** and **Polygamy in Islamic Law** for Dr. Gamal Badawi, **Women in Islam and Muslim Society** for Dr. Hasan Turabi, **Feminism and Muslim Women** for Sajda Nazlee, **The Place of Women in Islamic Life** for Dr. Yusuf al Qaradawi, and **Women Between Islam and Western Society** for Maulana Wahududdin Khan. Please refer to the reference section of this book for a more exhaustive list on works about women in Islam. These books have enriched the Islamic library and provided much needed material for Muslims and non Muslims alike to understand the true position of Muslim women in Islam.

On the other hand, many unfair writers, orientalists as well as secular Muslims and supporters of the feminist movement, have tried to condemn Islam and label it as demeaning, humiliating, and unjust towards women. They have accused Islam unjustifiably by saying that its teachings encourage the mistreatment of women and favour the male gender over the female, which is far from the truth. In the recent years, with the increase in domestic violence, particularly in North America and among Muslim families, these writers also incorrectly tried to link this increase to the concept of *qawamah*. Let me say it loud and clear, our faith has no room for domestic violence, but unfortunately some Muslims are committing it, sometimes in a fit of rage, or as a way to resolve marital conflicts. This is completely unacceptable from an Islamic point of view and is strongly condemned by Muslim scholars, leaders, and community activists alike. Islam should not be held hostage for the behaviour of certain ignorant and disobedient Muslims

To shed more lights on this issue we would like the reader to consider the following facts linked with the analysis presented by various scholars in the previous section:

• The two most important foundations of the spousal relationship in Islam are *Mawadah*[78] and *Rahmah*[79], as stated in the **Qur'an**[80]

• In many places in the **Qur'an**, Allah *SWT* advises husbands to treat their wives in a very kind and dignified way, even during the most difficult times of a relationship, such as times of separation and divorce[81]

• Numerous teachings of Prophet Muhammad *SAAW* emphasized being gentle and kind in all dealings and particularly in the marital relationship. Here are some examples:

– "Kindness is not found in anything, but it adds beauty to it, and if it withdrawn from anything, it defects it"[82]

– "Those who are deprived of leniency are deprived of all good"[83]

– "Allah is kind and He loves kindness in all affairs"[84]

– "Allah is kind and He loves kindness; and confers upon kindness which He does not confer upon severity and does not confer upon anything else besides it (kindness)."[85]

– "A believing man (husband) must not dislike a believing woman (his wife). If he dislikes one of her traits, he should remember that there are other traits that he likes."[86]

---

[78] *Mawadah* emphasizes a deeper sense of love with gentle and kind treatment which brings the best behaviour out of the person and the relationship and contributes to the righteousness of both spouses

[79] *Rahamah* means compassion, leniency, and kindness

[80] (Q30, V21)

[81] (Q2, V228, V231, V233), (Q4, V19)

[82] Muslim

[83] Muslim

[84] Agreed upon

[85] Muslim

[86] Muslim

– "The believers who show the most perfect faith are those who have the best character and the best of you are those who are best to their wives."[87]

– "The best of you is he who is best to his family, and I'm the best among you to my family."[88]

• Prophet Muhammad *SAAW* used to be in the process of serving his family, but when prayer was called, he would go out for prayer.[89]

The above is obvious testimony that Islam promotes a kind, positive, and healthy relationship between husband and wife. The spirit of the spousal relationship in Islam is that of compassion and cooperation, for the good and the wellbeing of the family in particular and the society in general. Islam doesn't promote a spirit of ill treatment, hatred, and violence; far from it. However, to achieve the positive spirit of kindness sought for, both husband and wife have to work together in understanding the concept of *qawamah* properly, and purifying and cleansing their souls.[90]

Some may argue these points, asking how this fits with the **Qur'an**'s use of the word *daraba*[91] as one of the means to deal with the wife in the case of *nushooz*[92], as stated in the *qawamah* verse.[93]

Here is our response to this argument:

• The word *daraba* was used in **Qur'an** to indicate many meanings, as the analysis of Dr. Abusulayman showed in the previous section.[94] The meaning he selected is for the husband to distance himself from his wife if the first and the second stage suggested in the verse of resolving the

---

[87] At-Termezi

[88] At-Termezi

[89] Al Bukhari

[90] See chapter 7 of our book, **Blissful Marriage,** New edition published by amana publications, Beltsville, Maryland, USA, 2005

[91] *Daraba* as an Arabic word has many meanings. See the analysis of Dr. Abusulayman in the previous section of this book

[92] See the detailed meaning of the word *nushooz* in the previous section

[93] (Q4, V34)

[94] See reference number 27

conflict doesn't work out. The next stage after this would be for family arbitration, as suggested in verse 35 of *surah al-Nisa'*. This is a very legitimate understanding and it fully agrees with the spirit of human dignity promoted by Islam in all areas of life, and particularly in family relationships as we indicated above

• Another meaning of the word *daraba* in the Arabic language is to have the very close intimate relations that take place between married couples.[95] A husband would first use the two stages described in the verse. He would admonish his wife (the stage of *mawe'zah*) first, then he would refuse to share her bed (*Hajr fi al Madaje'*) with the purpose of making the wife realize the gravity of the situation and the seriousness of its consequences for a certain period of time. After this, he would be able to return to having intimate relation with his wife. This intimate act, particularly after a period of abstinence due to an existing conflict, is known to bring spouses very close to each other and could open the door for gentle discussion, which may help in easing the tension and resolving the disagreement.

• As for those who insist that the meaning of the verb *daraba* in this context is to hit or inflict physical pain, before using the verse as permission, we remind them with the following:

– Prophet Muhammad *SAAW* never hit with his hand either a servant or a woman, but, of course, fought in the cause of Allah. He never took revenge on anyone for torture inflicted on him, but, of course, exacted retribution for the sake of Allah when the injunctions of Allah were violated.[96]

– Prophet Muhammad *SAAW*, on many occasions, advised the believers to be kind to their womenfolk and not to hit them.

– According to majority of scholars, the three stages described in the verse should only be used if the *nushooz* is **certain**

– The degree of the authenticity of the *hadeeth* mentioned under the section "General Interpretation of the Verse" on page 15 , which related the verse to an incident where a husband hit his wife, is doubtful, to say the least

---

[95] See reference 20

[96] Muslim

I couldn't find this *hadeeth* in any of the nine books of Al-Bukhary, Muslim, Al-Termezey, Abu Dawood, Al-Nesae'y, Ibn Majah, Ahmad, Malek, and Al-Darmey

– The husband can not use the third stage of the process before exhausting the first two stages. This means that he should not use his hand to hit or inflict physical pain on his wife before admonishing her first and staying away from her in bed for a period that could range from one month to four months. If the first two stages are to be followed properly, then certainly, by the time the third stage is to be applied, the husband will be completely calm and may not at all hit his wife

– As Sh. Muhammad Al Ghazaly said, "looking closely at the *Sunnah* of the Prophet *SAAW*, however, I cannot find a justification for this last measure (*darb*) except when the wife refuses vehemently and persistently to engage in intimate relations with her husband, or when she brings male outsiders into their home in the absence of her husband, both of which represent, as we can see, very serious problems indeed."

– Even if he decided to apply the third stage after a month or four months, it is symbolic at this time, and he must observe certain etiquettes in administering this disciplinary measure such as:

• Using a very soft object such as a tooth brush or a miswak
• Avoiding the face
• Not yelling, shouting, humiliating, or calling bad names during the process.

Considering the above, it is clear that the process recommended by the verse of qawamah is very gentle and has nothing to do with domestic violence. It is completely different and can't be compared to domestic violence in any way. Domestic violence is usually resorted to as the first option to resolve the conflict by those who practice it. It is done in a fit of rage and has nothing to do with *qawamah*.

So what could then be the reason for the increase in domestic violence among Muslims, particularly living in the West, in the recent years?

Family Leadership (Qawamah)

Abdul Malik Mujahid, a known Muslim activist and the founder of Sound Vision[97], in his letter that he shared with the Chicago Muslim community after the CEO and founder of Bridges TV had reportedly killed his wife and turned himself in to the Buffalo, NY Police Department, shares the following words of wisdom regarding domestic violence:

> "Domestic violence is connected with pressure. Hassans (name of CEO of Bridges TV) were going through divorce and their business Bridges TV was not doing good according to media reports. A Muslim social service leader told me in Ramadan that she sees more cases of domestic violence than in other months. That seems very possible to me, since other reports have linked the Christmas season in the U.S. with high domestic violence. Pressure as well as stress, depression, and anxiety is linked to domestic violence.

> I'm sharing these painful thoughts with the rest of you, in order to request our *Masjid* leadership and imams to address the subject of domestic violence in their communities. Just last week when I was giving a *khutbah* at MCC, there was a funeral taking place. It was for a young man who was just 30 years old. He had been depressed, and had died from an overdose of medicine. Just a few days ago a Chicagoan Mustafa Mustafa hurt his girlfriend while visiting LA before leading police on a chase and then committing suicide. Probably many of you remember how sister Shahpara was burned to death in Northside Chicago.

> There have been more than a few cases in the recent past in which Muslims in America have killed people around them. At least two of them were taking medicine for depression.

---

[97] He is currently the president of Sound Vision's board of directors

According to a **USA Today** report, more than 50% of Arab Americans have clinical signs of depression. And when you separate them from Arabs of other religions, 70% of MuslimArab Americans have clinical signs of depression. Although I have not talked to the Yale University scholar about her methodology for this survey, I believe these signs of clinical depression are not exclusive to Arab Muslims. It corresponds to the hints of depression I see in our community all around me.

I think it is most likely connected with what Muslims have gone through after the attacks on September 11. Half a million Muslims, for instance, were interviewed by the FBI. And now with the increasingly bad economic signs, everyone is under some degree of stress.

Know that domestic violence is prevalent throughout the country, and that depression is not something Muslims have a monopoly on. But I fear that the rate of depressed Muslims is higher than in the general community. So my request is the following: our newsletters, imams, *khatibs, halaqahs*, our weekend schools, and our adult weekend programs should emphasize the following in their programs:

• Spirituality, so their relationship with God can be a source of strength

• We should make the literature on depression, stress, anger management available in our newsletters and mailing lists.

• Good numbers of *khutbahs* and *halaqahs* should focus on these issues so Muslims are better equipped to handle this issue in their community.

• We need to strengthen the family support system by pre-marriage counselling, through marriage mediation, and conflict resolution techniques. This can be gained through strengthening Muslim social service agencies.

• Offer anger management classes to brothers.

• Sisters groups should have *halaqas* on the rights of women and methods of handling these situations.

By researching close to 50 books on violence in late 90s, I learned that there is a direct link between frustration and aggression. As the economic situation gets worse, the domestic violence will increase and that is why I feel that we need to prepare ourselves so we can prevent and mediate frustration and depression so it doesn't lead to violence. [98]

May Allah keep all of us mentally healthy and in a relationship with Allah which enriches us with the respect and rights of our loved one.

Peace."

– Abdul Malik Mujahid

In addition to the above analysis and wonderful suggestions of Dr. Mujahid, we also emphasize the importance of the proper understanding of Islamic teachings, particularly in the area of family relations. It is of paramount importance that National Muslim organizations and local Imams offer marriage workshops that not only stress the foundation of marriage in Islam, but also cover both pre-marital and marital counseling with very clear practical examples. Availability of literature on family matters that is relevant to the North American environment is another crucial area where Muslim scholars, Imams, and activists should collaborate to make it easily available and accessible to, at least, Muslims living in this part of the world.

---

[98] See Sound Vision's page on Domestic Violence and Muslims: http://www.soundvision.com/info/ domesticviolence /

Appropriate Use of *Qawamah*

INTRODUCTION

I n this section we will provide many practical examples illustrating the appropriate use of *Qawamah*. We will try to make sure that we cover as many areas as possible of married couples' lives in general, and those who live in North America in particular. Our goal is to make sure that by the end of this section, the reader will better understand the proper, correct, and appropriate use of *Qawamah* and realize that it covers many areas of day-to-day interactions among married couples.

CAMPUS CALLS

Laiyla and Lotfi have been married for 9 months. As the couple married young, Laiyla is still finishing her undergraduate degree. One evening, Laiyla has to go to her university campus for an important group meeting for one of her course projects. Laiyla takes the metro to campus and attends the meeting with the rest of her group at the university library. The meeting runs a little late and Laiyla finds that it is almost 10:45pm by the time they are done the meeting. She calls Lotfi on his cell phone to find that he is still at his office, working late. Lotfi tells her to wait for him in the library and that he will come pick her up once he is finished sending an important email to a client. Laiyla replies that if she heads out now and takes the metro home it will only take her 20 minutes and she will be home before he's even finished the email. She explains to him that they've both had a long day and that it would be easier for both of them if she just took the metro home instead of having to wait for him and have him make the trip all the way down to her campus from his office and then go back home. But Lotfi insists that it's not safe for her to take the metro at this hour alone and asks her to please just wait for him to come pick her up. "I know you're tired dear, but it's better to be safe than sorry. Maybe you could read a book until I come."

Laiyla agrees to wait for him and decides to check her email in the library until he comes.

Why it is appropriate:

• Lotfi's request that Laiyla not take public transportation at 11pm is reasonable because many big cities' public transportation and metro systems aren't very safe at that hour, and Lotfi is in charge of protecting Laiyla's safety.

• Even though what Lofti did required sacrifice from him and extra time and effort, he did the right thing because it is part of his duty as a husband to look out for the well-being of his wife and be concerned about her security.

• Lotfi offers Laiyla an alternative solution to her idea which is that he will come and pick her up, which will only mean that she will have to wait on campus for a little while longer.

WHEN IT RAINS IT POURS

Hanan and Mustafa are happily married. They don't have any kids yet but are hoping from Allah *SWT* to have some in the near future, especially since Hanan has recently finished her university studies. As a matter of fact, Hanan also wants some work experience, particularly before she becomes busy with having kids. One day, Hanan raises the issue of applying to work with Mustafa and he happily welcomes it. They both agree that the job she starts should not take her away from her other commitments between house work, spending quality time with Mustafa and being active in her local community.

Hanan applies for work in her field and before she knows it, she's working 20 to 25 hours a week in a nearby private company. The first few weeks of Hanan's shift in lifestyle takes some adjusting from both spouses, but it is something they have prepared for and Mustafa is very understanding. A little over a month down the road, Hanan gets a phone call from a company she had applied to when she was on the job hunt. It turns out to be a well-respected, multinational corporation inviting her for an interview for a half-day weekend job. She quickly becomes excited about it, as working for such a company would look really good on her resume, and best of all, there would not be any time conflict with her current job.

That evening over dinner, Hanan tells Mustafa about her new job offer and how it's a rare opportunity to work for such a company. She also makes a commitment that if she were to start that weekend job, it would not affect her other obligations, particularly because it would only take a few more hours from her every week. However, Mustafa raises a few important points that Hanan was overlooking. He reminds her that such a weekend job could deter their ability to fulfill their social commitments and perhaps reduce her ability to attend her weekly committee meetings at the weekend Islamic school.

After attending the interview and receiving an offer of employment, Hanan has one more lengthy discussion with Mustafa about working for the multinational company. Hanan still insists that she should not miss this rare opportunity. Mustafa on the other hand does not agree with her reasoning and tries to convince her that her current job is sufficient for the time being and that it would still look good on her resume. He makes it clear to her that if she really wants to accept her new offer that she would have to quit her current job.

Why it is appropriate:

• At the start of her job hunt, Hanan and Mustafa both agreed that the job she starts should not take her away from her other commitments between house work, spending quality time with Mustafa and being active in her local community. Mustafa is reminding Hanan of this commitment, which she will probably not be able to keep by starting a second job on the weekend.

• If Hanan starts this second job, she will probably not be able to keep her work/life/community balance intact because there is no such thing as superwoman and thus one of these areas will no doubt suffer a bit.

• Muslims are supposed to live balanced lives and fulfill their responsibilities toward all who have a right upon them. Though it is fine for Hanan to build and succeed in her career, she also shouldn't neglect her husband, family and community's needs and rights upon her.

THE DEAD END JOB

Abbas is a hard working husband. He has a reasonable position with a high tech firm in a small town. He has been living with his wife Sayedah and his two young children in this small town for the last ten years. Sayedah has developed good relationships with several families in the area and become good friends with them. They get together regularly for various activities and they visit each other often. She is very happy with these friendships and considers most of them as her family since she doesn't have any family living close by.

Abbas has been working with the same firm for the last ten years and is still in the same position. He has been trying hard to move up the ladder, but his attempts haven't borne any fruit in spite of all his efforts. He feels that there is no future for him in this firm. He has been talking to Sayedah for the last couple of years, who has been asking him to be patient and try harder. Recently, and after a long discussion with Sayedah, he decided to look for a job elsewhere. He started sending his resume to various firms with the hope of finding a better position, even if it is in another city. After a few interviews with various hiring managers at different companies, he finally received an attractive offer from one firm in a completely different State. In addition to a considerable increase in his salary, the potential of moving to a higher position in the company is very real. The offer also included a trip for his family to the company's location to check out the new city, look for a new house, and find out if they will be happy moving to this new location. Abbas and Sayedah took the trip and together took a tour of the city, found out that there is more than one Islamic center in town, and visited a few of these centers. They also checked the schooling for their children and they found more than one good school in the vicinity of Abbas's new work place.

Abbas is very happy with this new opportunity and thinks it would be very good to accept the offer. However, whenever he discusses the matter with Sayedah to finalize his response, she says: "I don't want to move to a new place where I have no friends. It will be so hard and I will miss all my good friends. It will take so long to find the same kind of friends in this new place." Abbas tries to convince Sayedah that the new place has a bigger Muslim community, and the new position also has many advantages that will reflect positively on the whole family. However, she is not fully convinced because of the friendship issue.

Abbas knows that the decision can't be put off forever, and that as the head of the family he must be the one who makes it, as he is entrusted by Allah *SWT* to provide, protect, take care of, and be responsible for his family affairs. At this point, it is clear that Abbas has fulfilled the requirements of *Qawamah* in terms of doing the proper research and consulting with his family members before finalizing the decision. If Abbas decides to move the family to the new location and accept the new job offer, even with Sayedah not fully convinced, he is using *Qawamah* properly and Sayedah should accept his decision and help him and the family to start this new stage of their lives.

Why it is appropriate:

• Though Sayedah's apprehensions about moving are understandable, there would also be many benefits to this move for the entire family, and the advantages of moving in this case outweigh the disadvantages.

• Abbas and Sayedah have discussed the issue thoroughly and have even taken a trip to the new city to make sure it would be suitable for the children and provide a positive Islamic environment.

• Sometimes we have to take a step that is outside our comfort zone to reap certain benefits for ourselves and for our family.

• The **Qur'an** and Islam promote and encourage traveling through out the earth and reflecting on other's cultures, even if it will require some adjustment on our part.

Hajj is in the Air

Mariam and Ali got married last year in the Middle East and recently moved to Canada for Ali's work. Mariam really misses her family and looks forward to visiting them every summer. Mariam and Ali go home the first summer for a long visit and have a wonderful trip. After they return to Canada, they decide to discuss their spiritual goals and make some commitments to things they want to do as a couple. They agree to study Quran together weekly and each read some every day, as well as deciding that they want to seriously save up for Hajj, with a plan to do it as soon as possible. When they sit down to look at their finances, they find that their biggest expense would be their yearly visit to the Middle East. Ali says that, in order to really be able to save for Hajj, they should visit every two or three years instead of each summer. Mariam disagrees. She says that she misses her family too much to wait that long to see them. Ali reminds Mariam that she hasn't yet adjusted to life in Canada, and that as soon as she has gotten to know some new friends, it will help her get over how much she misses her family. He also reminds her how important Hajj is, and how they should really try to do it while they still have the chance. Mariam says she knows it's important, but that it's hard being so far away from her family.

The next day, Ali surprises Mariam with a gift of an internet phone account so she can call her family whenever she wants. He tells her that he hopes that talking to them a lot will help her feel closer to them even though they're far away, and that he knows it will be difficult at first, but that he's decided that saving up for Hajj is the higher priority, and that they won't be going to visit next year. He also tells her that he will make more of an effort to help her get to know other sisters in her new community so she can begin to build friendships here and fill some of the void of moving so far from her family. He promises to take her to sister's halaqas and community events and introduce her to all his friend's wives so that she has more of an opportunity of meeting new friends.

Why it is appropriate:

• Hajj is one of the pillars of Islam and is an obligation upon every Muslim who has the financial and physical ability to go. Therefore, it is worth the sacrifice of not taking other trips to visit family for a temporary period of time until this fard is completed.

• It was considerate of Ali to realize how difficult it is for his wife to be far away from her family and not have the opportunity to visit them for a while, and to buy her an internet phone card that would allow her to talk to them as often as she likes and help to minimize her homesickness.

• Ali is going to do his best to help Mariam get to know other sisters in her new community so that she can build new friendships in her new city.

ONE CAR IS BETTER THAN TWO

Sarah and Marwan are a very busy couple. They both work full time in two different parts of the city and share one car to get to work, with Marwan dropping Sarah off each morning and picking her up each evening on the way home. Marwan and Sarah both agreed early in their marriage that Sarah would contribute part of her income toward their expenses for running the household. Last year, they started saving up for a second car so that they could spend less time on their commute and have more time to spend together as a couple. They've been saving well and now have half of the money they need to buy the car.

One day after Friday prayer, one of the mosque administrators makes an important announcement. He tells the congregation that the mosque was recently examined by city inspectors, and that several infrastructure problems were found with the building. Unless repairs are undertaken soon, the city will shut the building down. Mosque administration is calling on everyone in the community to donate whatever they can to help save the mosque. They have only one week to raise a substantial amount of money to keep the mosque, which is the only large mosque in town, and has been serving the community for 20 years.

All afternoon, the problem bothers Marwan, and when he picks Sarah up from work that afternoon, he tells her about it. He's been thinking about it for a few hours, and he tells her he'd like to donate half their car savings. Sarah agrees that it's a good idea to donate some of the money but thinks half is probably too much. Marwan points out that their current car works fine and doesn't need repairs, and that getting the second car is really more a matter of convenience than it is urgent. They agree to sleep on the idea and discuss it again in the morning.

The next day, Sarah says she still feels that half the amount would be too much, and suggests donating a quarter of their car savings instead. Marwan disagrees. He says that the Muslim community in their town is well meaning, but not necessarily very wealthy, and that since so much money needs to be raised, even if many families donate, he's afraid that the mosque administration still won't meet its target. Marwan feels that they are in a good position to part with the money, while other people might want to donate a lot but not be able to afford it.

Over the course of the week, they continue to weigh the pros and cons of donating half the car savings. On one hand, they will be helping the mosque and earning good deeds insha'a Allah. On the other hand, donating such a substantial amount means it will take them an extra year to save for the car. By the end of the week, Sarah still feels that half the savings is too much, while Marwan still feels that it's a good amount to donate. Sarah indicates to Marwan that donating a quarter the amount for now is good enough and will allow them to buy the second car soon, which will give them more time together, while at the same time helping the mosque ensure its financial stability in the future. She also suggested that they can donate a quarter of the savings for now and monitor the situation. If there is a need for more, they will donate more later insha'a Allah. Marwan tells Sarah that he thinks this is a good idea, and that he thinks they should go with her suggestion. He thanks her for coming up with this idea and she thanks him for consulting with her, and for his willingness to compromise his position. Marwan also reminds Sarah and himself both to renew their intentions as they make the donation so that they may get the full reward from Allah *SWT*.

Why it is appropriate:

• Donating money or time for the sake of Allah is very important in Islam and Allah *SWT* rewards this act greatly. We also know that charity does not decrease wealth. Spouses are supposed to encourage each other to donate as much as they can for the sake of Allah. This is very important aspect of family life. Scholars point out that spouses helping each other to be closer to Allah *SWT* is one of the main objectives of marriage.

• Marwan didn't make the decision on his own. He consulted with Sarah and both discussed the pros and cons of each choice. Marwan didn't force Sarah to accept his position without questioning and thinking about various aspects of the decision, as well as all the consequences

• Considering Sarah's suggestion is a very positive and healthy move from Marwan. He not only consulted with her, but was also willing to change his own view on the matter and consider her views. This is a wonderful example demonstrating a healthy level of applying *Shura* in family life.

• Marwan reminded himself and Sarah to renew and purify their intentions as they donate the money. This shows that he is concerned that she gets the reward of the donation from Allah and is not just ordering her around.

ANY PLANS?

Rasheedah is an educated and responsible young woman who thinks that she is capable and mature. Her husband, Ahmad, is an educated professional who respects her and encourages her in her endeavours. Ahmad is working full time, while Rasheedah is finishing her university degree. They try to coordinate their schedules so that they always see each other during the weekdays.

One Sunday morning, after they've had breakfast together, they begin to get ready for their day. Ahmad is off to play sports with a few of his friends.

"What are you going to play?" Rasheedah asks.

"Ah, we haven't decided yet. Maybe basketball. Maybe soccer."

"Well, have fun," she says as she hugs him at the door.

"Assalaamu alaikum, Dear," he says.

"Wa'alaikum assalaam," she answers, closing the door behind him.

With the table cleared and Ahmad out, Rasheedah thinks this will be a perfect time to get started on that research paper that she has to work on for her history class. She settles into her desk chair, with her books and notes arranged around her, and opens up her file. She is focused, working for about an hour when the phone rings.

"Hello."

It's her friend Suad who is with her in history class. She lives only a few blocks away and she invites Rasheedah over so they can work on their papers together. "I could really use some motivation, really Rasheedah, come on over. It'll be so much easier to go through this torture together!"

"You're right. My will was weakening and I was seriously considering going out for a walk. Or cooking," Rasheedah confesses.

"You were thinking of cooking at 10 in the morning." Both girls laugh. "You need to get over here," Suad commands.

Rasheedah thinks it's a good idea. She packs up her books & notes and emails her file to herself. She glances at her watch. Ahmad isn't expected home before 2 p.m. 'I have four hours,' she thinks to herself. 'That's plenty of time.' She grabs her stuff and heads out. At Suad's place, the two women work and push each other on. At one o'clock Rasheedah gathers her things, thanks Suad for her encouragement, and heads home. On her walk home she's rather pleased with herself and how much she was able to accomplish in the three hours at Suad's house. She comes back home feeling positive & decides to get some lunch started so her and Ahmad can eat together when he gets back. She finishes preparing lunch just as Ahmad is coming in.

"Perfect timing," she calls out. "Lunch is hot!"

"Oh terrific!" he exclaims.

They sit down to lunch and have a great meal. Both of them are in a good mood and the conversation is great.

"It's amazing how much motivation you can get just from knowing that you're not alone," Rasheedah remarks. "I mean, this morning I worked by myself for an hour on that research paper and I was just about ready to quit. But then Suad called and I went over to work with her and I kept at it for three hours! Can you believe it? I got so much done Alhamdulillah. I'm just so happy about it!"

"You went over to Suad's this morning?" Ahmad asks.

"Yeah," she answers, "and got a whole lot done! *Alhumdulillah!*"

"You didn't tell me you were going out," Ahmad remarks.

"Well, yeah. I wasn't planning on it. But I'm glad I went. What's wrong Ahmad?" Rasheedah asks.

"Well, I didn't think you'd just go over to someone's house without letting me know," he answers.

"It's not 'somebody's house'. It's Suad's house. She's not a stranger, Ahmad."

"I know. I'm not saying don't go. I'm just saying, let me know."

"Ahmad, I don't understand," says Rasheedah, the annoyance starting to show in her voice.

"Well, I'd just like you to tell me if you're planning to go to anyone's house. That's all."

Rasheedah stares at him. She feels insulted. 'I'm 22.' She thinks. 'I'm not a kid.'

"It's just a safety thing," Ahmad says. "I need to know where you are. If you're at someone's house, I'd like to know."

Rasheedah sits quietly. Inside, she's fuming.

Why it is appropriate:

• Ahmad is not asking Rasheedah not to go out of the house at all, he's just asking her to let him know if she plans on going out, or decides to go out so that he knows where she is in case of an emergency. This seems reasonable, because he is responsible for her safety and thus should know where she is. If something were to happen to her, God forbid, and Ahmad had no idea where she was at all, it would make it much more difficult to find her.

• Ahmad and Rasheedah could agree that, if Rasheedah doesn't plan to go out, but something comes up last minute and she wants/needs to go out when she can't reach Ahmad to tell him, she could leave him a message on his cell phone or work answering machine to let him know where she is going and when she expects to be back.

LOOKING GOOD…TOO GOOD!

One evening, Hamzah and his wife Aisha were getting ready to go out to a community fundraising dinner for the mosque that the community was trying to build. They had already gotten the two boys ready. When Aisha came out of the room, Hamzah stopped dead in his tracks. "You're wearing that?" he questioned.

"What?" she asked. "You don't think it looks good?"

"Well no. It looks good - too good for outside. That's the problem."

"What's the problem?" she asked. "I'm not supposed to look bad outside."

"No, but the shirt is a bit too tight," he explained.

Aisha stared at him. "You didn't say that last time I wore it."

"Look I don't remember when you wore it. All I know is that it's too tight now. I don't think you should go out in that."

"Then what am I supposed to wear?" she demanded.

"Anything else in your closet," he suggested.

Aisha sighed and went back into their room. She took a look in the mirror and felt that she looked good. So it was a little tight. So what? It wasn't as tight as other women wore all the time. Besides, it was such a nice outfit. She changed into another outfit. 'How uninspiring!' she thought. 'The blue shirt was much nicer!"

They went out to the fundraising dinner, but Aisha was quiet and distant all night. When they got home they barely said a word before getting into bed. Before they went to sleep, Hamzah gave it one last shot.

"Aisha, I know you're upset about me telling you not to go out in the blue shirt," he started. "But you have to understand that it's my responsibility for you not to do anything that would displease Allah. What would I say to Allah on the day of Judgment?"

Why it is appropriate:

• It is both spouses' responsibility (and all sisters and brothers responsibility) to give each other naseeha (advice) to help each other avoid doing anything that would displease Allah and this is what Hamzah was doing. The Prophet Mohamed (*SAAW*) tells us: "The Muslim is the mirror of his brother/of her sister" which means that we should help each other change for the better by advising each other kindly in religious matters.

I Want My Mommy

Lena and Khaled have been married for 2 years and have recently been making *dua*' that Allah (*SWT*) bless them with children. A few months later, to their delight, Lena discovers that she is pregnant. She tells Khaled the exciting news and the two celebrate happily and thank Allah (*SWT*) for all His blessings. A few weeks into the pregnancy, Lena starts to feel very sick. She feels tired and weak all the time and is constantly nauseous and vomiting. The sight of most food completely disgusts her and she can smell odd scents from what feels like miles away! In short, she's experiencing the typical symptoms of pregnancy. Khaled helps as much as he can while working full time by bringing her snacks and meals whenever he's at home and helping prepare light meals for their dinner. However, with his full time work, it gets a bit difficult for him to keep up with all her needs. Since Lena's parents live in a nearby city, Lena thinks it might be a good idea for her to go stay with her mom and dad for a few weeks, just until she gets over the most difficult period of pregnancy. She suggests this idea to Khaled one night. After thinking about it for a while and praying salat al istikhara, Khaled agrees that, if this is what will make Lena feel better at this time, then she can go and stay with her parents for a few weeks to make this difficult period easier on her. "But I'll definitely miss having you around", he adds. Lena thanks him for his kindness and understanding and the next weekend, the two drive down to her parent's nearby city together. Khaled stays for the weekend and Lena stays for five weeks, during which time Khaled comes and visits her frequently. While Lena is at her parent's place, they very kindly prepare her meals and bring her food and try to make her as comfortable as possible. Lena is very grateful to both her parents and Khaled for their support and understanding at this time.

Why it is appropriate:

• Khaled was very understanding of Lena's needs and feelings during this time and did what he felt was in her and the growing baby's best interest as opposed to only considering his own wants and desires.

• Khaled took into account the fact that Lena's parents might be able to do a better job of providing for Lena's needs at this time because they have more experience in these matters and don't work as many hours as Khaled, and thus can be around Lena more.

Inappropriate Use of *Qawamah*

INTRODUCTION

Again, in this section we will provide many practical examples illustrating the inappropriate use of *Qawamah*. We will try to make sure that we cover as many areas of married couples' lives as possible. The examples will relate to married couples in general and those who live in North America in particular. Our goal is to make sure that the reader clearly understands the improper, wrong, and inappropriate use of *Qawamah* and realizes that its spectrum covers many areas of day-to-day interactions among married couples.

I'VE MADE MY DECISION, END OF DISCUSSION!

"Khaleel is happily married to Saleema. They have two children who are of school age. He just started a new job with a new company a few months ago. As such, he is only allowed to take two vacation weeks every year. Last year and the year before, the whole family spent their holidays visiting Khaleel's parents who live in a nearby state. Saleema's parents live in Europe, and alhamdulellah to her advantage (she thought), there is a direct flight between the city they live in and her parents' city in Europe.

Since Khaleel just joined this new firm a few months ago, he can't take his vacation until after the start of the school year. Saleema was hoping to visit her parents during summer vacation this year, since the last time they visited was over three years ago. Saleema suggested to Khaleel that she, with the children, could visit her parents over summer vacation. His response was, "No. We should wait until next summer and we can all go together."

Saleema begged him to allow her and the children to go this summer because her parents are old and her father particularly is sick, as well as the fact that she hasn't seen them for over three years. Khaleel said, "No, I don't feel comfortable with you traveling alone. I know it is safe and it is only one flight without stopovers or connections, but I still don't feel comfortable with this arrangement."

63

Saleema tried every possible way she could think of to convince *Khaleel*, but he adamantly refused to discuss the issue further, saying, "I've made my decision. You are not traveling this summer. End of discussion."

Why it is inappropriate

• Khaleel does not give his wife a chance to discuss the matter with him and decides on his own that she and the children cannot go without seriously considering the pros and cons of such a situation.

• He quickly dismisses his wife's need and duty to see her aging and sick parents and spend time with them (birr al walidayn).

• The transportation arrangements available (direct flight) pose no safety issues for her and the children and yet he refuses.

THERE'S NOTHING MORE TO DISCUSS

Assia and Arif have been married for 2 and a half years. Since the beginning of their marriage, Assia has been a homemaker and Arif has been working for an engineering firm. The two do not have any kids yet. After three years of staying at home, Assia approached Arif one evening and said that there was something she would like to speak to him about. So the two sat down together after dinner and Assia explained to Arif that she would like to go back to work. She would like to put her pharmacy degree to good use and try to see if she can find a job in her field. Arif listened carefully and then asked, "Are you unsatisfied with the income I bring in?" Assia tried to explain that her desire to go back to work had nothing to do with the amount of money he earns, but that she would like to feel more fulfilled and fill her free time by working. Arif nodded and said, "I need some time to think this over." After thinking about it for a few days, Arif told Assia that he had decided that her working would be a bad idea. He said he was uncomfortable with the idea of her interacting with men at the workplace and was afraid it would cause fitna in their marriage. Needless to say, Assia was not pleased with his decision and asked him to reconsider. "I'm sorry but my mind is already made up," he replied. Assia asked if they could at least discuss this more, so that they could work around the issues that were making Arif uncomfortable. But Arif's only response was, "There's nothing more to discuss."

Why it is inappropriate:

• The husband did not even give himself and his wife a fair chance of really discussing the issue. His concerns may be valid but they also may have feasible solutions (such as choosing a good work environment, interacting professionally with men, not working at late hours etc.)

• According to Islam, consultation is an integral component of family life and it is the duty of the husband to consult with all family members, particularly his wife, regarding family decisions. It is clear in this case that Arif did not exhaust the means of consultation with his wife regarding this issue.

THAT'S IMPOSSIBLE, I'M HIS WIFE

Imran and Khawla have been married for 9 years and have 3 children. The family lives between Illinois, where the kids go to school, and Qatar where Imran has a good, high paying job. Imran usually visits the family in Chicago once a year for a few weeks when he has time off work, and Khawla and the kids usually travel to Qatar once or twice a year during the kids' vacation to be with Imran. Recently, Imran has been feeling very lonely in Qatar and feels it is difficult to live completely alone for so many months out of the year. However, he also feels that this situation is best for his family because he knows that he probably wouldn't have access to the same high paying job in North America. He also doesn't want to have to start over in a new country where he would have to reinvest many years networking and building work experience. Despite this, Imran can't escape the feelings of loneliness and boredom nagging at him. To solve his problem, Imran decides to marry a second wife in Qatar. He's unsure as to how Khawla will react, so he decides not to tell her right away. When his new wife, Bayan, asks him when he will inform his first wife, Imran replies by saying, "Not just yet. When the time is right, I will let her know." Then one evening, when Imran is out, Khawla calls him in Qatar and Bayan picks up the phone. Khawla is stunned to hear a female voice pick up the phone in her home. "Who is this?" she immediately demands.

"This is Imran's wife," Bayan replies.

"That's impossible, I'm his wife!"

"Well so am I," replies Bayan, "Aren't you going to welcome me to the family?"

Khawla can't believe her ears and is shocked that Imran could do such a thing behind her back.

Why it is inappropriate:

• Imran should have shared and discussed with his wife Khawla the fact that he is feeling lonely while living alone in Qatar. If he had opened up to his wife about his feelings, maybe the two of them together could have come up with a solution that was satisfactory to both, instead of the deceitful and hurtful action Imran ended up taking.

• By marrying a second wife behind his first wife's back, Imran completely broke his first wife's heart. He completely broke any trust that might exist between them and he probably caused lasting and deep resentment in their relationship (not to mention that he may have broken the family up if Khawla decides she will not accept this).

• Some scholars make it a requirement on the husband to inform his first wife of his intention to marry a second one before actually marrying her, and give the first wife the choice either to accept or to seek separation.

I'D JUST LIKE TO BE ABLE TO COME HOME TO A QUIET HOUSE AND RELAX

Kareema and Ahmed have been married for about a year. Kareema moved from another city to Ahmed's city after the wedding and is studying for her Master's degree, while Ahmed works full time. Ahmed has always been very involved in Islamic activities in his city. Kareema used to be very involved in Islamic activities in her old town, but has found that there aren't any activities for sisters here. She has looked for sisters' halaqas (study circles) or public lectures at university and at the mosque but can't find anything.

Kareema is starting to feel depressed about this and brings up the problem with some other sisters she has met at university. She's happy to find a few sisters who are interested in starting a halaqa with her, but unfortunately, they all live in different parts of the city and Kareema is the only one who lives in a central location that is easy to get to. Together, the girls discuss their schedules and find that the only possible times they are all available to meet is either Tuesday or Thursday night. Kareema tells the other girls she'll check with her husband about using their apartment for their halaqa, and if not, they can always try to book a room on a weekly basis at the university.

That night, over dinner, Kareema tells Ahmed about the halaqa idea excitedly, but Ahmed doesn't look happy about it. "I don't know, Kareema," he says, "I'm already so tired when I get home from work. I don't think I could stay out later on a week night."

"It's okay," Kareema answers. "You can come home and just go to our bedroom or the study. We'll just be in the living room."

Ahmed shakes his head. "It'll be too noisy. Honestly, I'd just like to be able to come home to a quiet house and relax."

Kareema tells Ahmed that the other possible location is on campus, but asks him if he can pick her up after the halaqa, since the bus from university to their building doesn't run past 8 p.m. and she doesn't drive. Ahmed tells her that he'd be too tired to come get her, and that he'd really rather they found a time during the day to do the halaqa, and then she could do it on campus or at their place. Kareema explains that a lot of the sisters study full time and wouldn't be able to make it during the day, and that this is really important to her, but Ahmed says it's just too hard, and that maybe next semester the schedules will work out and she'll be able to start a halaqa during the day.

"I can't honey. I'm just too tired after working all day."

Why it is inappropriate:

• Ahmed isn't considering Kareema's needs to socialize and gain knowledge with sisters

• It is the responsibility of the husband to provide the means for his family members to be educated, particularly in matters of religion

• The compromise Ahmed would have to make (ie going to their bedroom or the study one night a week while the women hold the halaqa in the living room) is really not unreasonable at all and is a very small price to pay to help his wife fulfill her social/educational needs.

DOUBLE DUTY, SINGLE EFFORT

Mona and Jalaal both work full time and have two children, 11 year-old Marwa, and 9 year-old Khalil. Mona has arranged a flexible schedule where she leaves for work early in the morning, so that she can be home when the kids get back from school at 4:30, while Jalaal's office is a bit further from their house and he returns home around 7pm. Mona's usual schedule is to get home, spend a bit of time with the children, get them started on their homework and then work in the kitchen to prepare the next day's food and clean up the kitchen or do laundry. Jalaal usually comes home from work very stressed and likes to unwind by watching sports for about an hour before the family has dinner.

Recently, Jalaal told Mona that he thinks the children need to be more focused while they do their homework, and that he'd like her to sit with them the whole time they're working on it, which would take about 2 hours every night. Mona says that she thinks the kids are doing quite well, and that she thinks their current system for homework is working, but Jalaal insists that they need more one-on-one attention. Mona points out that if she sits with the kids for 2 hours, to do their homework, she'll be starting the house chores much later in the evening, and won't have any time to do anything else before bed. She suggests that it would be more manageable if the two of them split homework duty. Jalaal gets irritated and tells her that by the time he gets home from such a long day, he's already exhausted and stressed from work, and that he needs to unwind, not sit with the kids to work on their homework. "I'm sure you can find the time to do it if you're more efficient," he tells her. "This is important."

Why it is inappropriate:

• Jalaal is insisting that Mona do something that he feels is important (and it may be) without considering Mona's opinion, time-constraints, and other responsibilities, and without being willing to give up any of his free time to make it work. If he really felt it was important, he would make himself available to help with it.

• Both Mona and Jalaal work full-time, yet it is only Mona's responsibility to take care of the housework, cooking and homework duty for their children, which is unfair.

• Although the mother is the main caregiver of the children according to Islam, most scholars agree that parenting is a joint and shared responsibility between both husband and wife. The prophet SAAW was always helping with house chores. Jalaal should be considerate and lend a helping hand to his wife.

YOU'RE NOT GOING. IT'S YOUR DUTY TO OBEY

Iman is a married woman with 2 kids, 6 and 8 years old. She lives in a small town outside Chicago, while her parents, two younger sisters, and one younger brother all live in Chicago. Iman's husband, Walid, works long hours and has an irregular schedule. One night, Iman told Walid that she wanted to go see her family on the weekend.

"You know how busy our weekends are," he responded.

"They're the only days that you don't work. What do you mean busy?" she asked.

"That's the only time I have to catch up on everything else. I need to sleep. To do the shopping. To read the paper. It's the only time I get to read the paper."

"Walid, come on. I really want to see them. My mom called today and she wants to see me."

Walid didn't say anything.

"Walid, can't we figure out a way to go this weekend?"

"I'll think about it," he responded. The next morning when Iman asked if he'd thought about it, Walid told her they couldn't go and told her about some of the things that he had to attend to this weekend.

"Well, what about next weekend?" she asked.

"We'll see," he said.

Iman shook her head as she walked out of the room. She felt hopeless about the situation. It had been bothering her for a while now. He never seemed to make the time to go visit her family.

That night Iman came up with the perfect solution. She could take the boys and go down to see her family on her own. They were only an hour's drive from her town and that way Walid's schedule would not be disturbed and she could still see her family. When she shared her idea with Walid he didn't seem nearly as excited about it as she was.

"Excuse me?" he asked. "You want to go out of town without me."

"It's not like I'm taking a vacation. I want to see my family."

"Without me?" he asked again. "It's out of the question. You're my wife and you don't travel without me."

"Walid, you don't have time to come with us and I don't want to see them once every two months. We have to find a way to work something out."

"There isn't a problem here, so we don't need to look for a solution," he stated.

"There is a problem!" she exclaimed.

"No, there isn't. You're overreacting."

"Walid –" Iman started.

"No, stop right there. I'm the man of the house and I've made my decision," he announced. "You're not going. It's your duty to obey."

Why it is inappropriate:

• Walid is not considering Iman's feelings and need to visit her family (silat al rahim and bir al walidayn)

• If Walid doesn't want to give up his weekend for the visit because it is the only relaxing time he gets, then he shouldn't hinder his wife from visiting her family and his kids from visiting their grandparents and aunts and uncles and building a strong relationship with them.

• There is nothing unsafe about Iman and the kids travelling alone to her parent's place (especially since they only live an hour away, and cell phones are widely available so all safety precautions could be arranged)

I'M A PERSON TOO!

Jameela is a 36-year-old woman living with her husband Hashem and her two pre-teen children. Jameela and Hashem have been married for 12 years and they get along quite well. All the same, Jameela feels isolated and wishes she could build strong friendships with other women, but can't figure out how. Whenever there is a get-together with any of the women she knows, she is invited, but when she tells Hashem about it, he seems always to disapprove. Feeling that she is becoming depressed and lonely, she decided to talk to her husband one day about a lunch coming up with some of her lady friends. "This time, I'll convince him," she thought. "I just have to go. . ."

"Hashem," she began one evening after the children had gone to bed, "there's something I would like to talk to you about."

Hashem turned to her and smiled.

"Aisha is having some women over for lunch on Tuesday insha'a Allah," she started. "It's a pot-luck and since the kids will be at school, well I thought it would be perfect. I could go and actually have adult conversation instead of being interrupted by the children every two minutes." She smiled broadly at him. But Hashem's smile had turned into a tight frown. His brows furrowed and he shook his head.

"We've already been over this, Jameela," he said quietly. "I don't know why you're bringing it up again."

"I just – aaaahhh. I can't keep going like this. I really need to see people."

"You see people. I'm a person, you're kids are people. The **Qur'an** lessons you go to, there are plenty of people there."

"No, it's different. I just want it to be light and social. I need that." Jameela explained.

"You don't need that. It's a waste of your time."

"Hashem, let's just try it, okay?"

"No, these women don't need you there. The kids need you. I need you. Your house needs you."

"What if I need them?" Jameela asked.

"You don't." Hashem replied. "You don't need them. What are you going to do? Sit and eat and talk. You can do that right here. You do it every day."

"Hashem, it's different."

"You're right. It's a waste of time."

Jameela stared at her husband in disbelief. "What about you and your soccer?" she asked.

"I'm exercising," he replied coolly.

Her cheeks flushed. "What about all the visiting you do? You meet your friends for coffee all the time. What's different about that?"

"We talk about important things. Women gossip. It's just not good. Don't go."

"I'm not going to gossip Hashem. I'm going to make friends. I really need some companionship!"

"I'm your companion, Jameela," Hashem said as he took her into a hug, trying to calm her down.

Jameela's heart was beating fast. She couldn't believe he didn't get it.

Why it is inappropriate:

• Hashem is being very insensitive and inconsiderate and he is not taking Jameela's natural need for female companionship and socialization into account. He is stopping her from doing something that is completely allowed in Islam if done in moderation.

• By socializing with her friends, Jameela will not be neglecting any of her duties as a mother or wife, so there is nothing wrong with her attending this lunch since it will not be at the expense of her children's well-being and it will fulfill a need of hers

• If Hashem is truly concerned that Jameela will be in a negative Islamic environment by attending the lunch because he is afraid the women will spend their time gossiping (which is a valid concern), then he should bring this point up and discuss it with Jameela. However, it's not fair of him to assume that all women do when they get together is gossip (though it is true that some women do this). He shouldn't ban Jameela from going just because this is a possibility, but could nicely ask her to beware of any gossip and try to change the subject or excuse herself early if that's what the main theme of the lunch ends up being.

• It is unfair of Hashem to allow himself the right of fulfilling his need to socialize with friends (by going out to coffee with them or playing sports with them) and then turn around and disallow Jameela the same right. The Qur'an indicates that women have the same rights as men. It declares, "And they (women) have rights similar to those (of men) over them, and men are a degree above them" [99]. If Jameela lets Hashem leave her alone so he can go socialize, it is also her right to socialize and he should provide her with this opportunity.

WHAT WERE YOU DOING ALL DAY?

Amani and Haitham have been married for 10 years and they have three children: a three year old son, a five year old daughter and an eight year old son. Haitham works full-time and Amani is staying at home to be with the children and tend to their needs. They both agreed to this arrangement happily and thought that it would be best for the family. However, Amani now feels undermined and hopeless when it comes to raising her children. It seems that she and Haitham have arguments about this subject on a daily basis.

On most days, Haitham doesn't see the children for more than an hour or two at the end of the day, but still he insists that he knows them and how to deal with them better. More often than not, when Amani is doing something with one of the children, whether it's helping them with their

---

[99] (Q2, V228)

homework, dressing them, or disciplining them, Haitham steps in and tells her how to do it. If the children are not dressed in their "home clothes", and finished their homework by the time he comes home from work, he questions Amani as to why they are not, and asks about every little thing they've done since they arrived from school. Amani doesn't mind that Haitham wants to be involved in raising the kids, she just wishes that he would talk about it less and actually get involved with them more. Haitham doesn't do much with the children. Even when he is going out to buy the groceries, he refuses to take one of the kids with him, saying that they slow him down in the store.

This issue has been lingering over them for some time, with Amani telling Haitham to help out more and Haitham insisting that he is helping out by telling her what to do. Two days ago though, it really exploded when they got into a heated argument. It started at the dinner table when their three year old son refused to eat his green peas.

"Okay, that's fine. Just finish up your other food, sweetie," Amani told their son as she spooned the green peas off of his plate and onto hers.

"What do you mean?" Haitham demanded, staring at Amani in disbelief."

"What?"

"Well, look at what you're teaching him! My God! You're spoiling the boy, Amani."

"Haitham, I just can't fight this right now, okay?"

"Oh, yeah. It's always about you. Never about what you're doing to the kid. 'Haitham I have a headache.' Or 'Haitham, I'm tired.' You act as if you're the only one who has any work to do. You know, at work, I can't just decide I don't want to do something. When are you going to start thinking of the kids Amani?"

Amani's face was red by this point and she was very upset.

"Don't talk to me like that!" she yelled.

"Don't yell at me Amani," Haitham said. "And don't tell me what to do."

"What's the big deal? What's the big deal anyway?" Amani asked, her voice lowered again. "I mean they're just a few green peas. What does it matter?"

"Oh, you are so short-sighted and narrow-minded."

"Don't start that with me. I'm his mother and I know him! It's just going to turn into a huge fight! And we're not going to win it, either."

"Well if you know him so well, why can't you get him to finish his plate?" Haitham challenged.

"Well, if you think it's so important, why don't you feed them to him?" Amani quipped, handing the plate of peas to Haitham.

"That's not my job." Haitham declared. "You're his mother."

Amani stood up with her other children who had finished eating while their parents argued. "Come on," she said to them. "Let's wash up and go finish your homework Ahmed."

"His homework's still not finished? What were you doing all day?"

Amani walked out of the room without looking at her husband.

Why it is inappropriate:

• Islamically, parenting is a shared responsibility. Though the mother is the main caregiver, the father should be involved (in more ways than just telling the mother what to do). If the father feels the mother is doing something wrong, he shouldn't undermine her authority and disrespect her in front of the children by confronting her in front of them, but, as with all advice-giving, he should bring up the issue with her nicely and in private and allow time for a discussion.

• Just because Haitham is the head of the family (qawwam) it doesn't mean he will automatically be an expert on any issue that the family faces, such as child psychology. If he really thinks that Amani is not raising the children properly or that she is using negative parenting techniques, then maybe they both need to educate themselves more on the issue of parenting by taking classes, attending workshops or reading good books on the topic.

• Haitham speaks in a disrespectful manner to his wife and does not follow the Islamic etiquettes of giving advice. Furthermore, he does this in front of the children, who will most likely model their father's negative behaviour. They will also disrespect their mother because of their father's attitude towards her.

STORY OF MY LIFE

Kawthar and Shafee are both in their mid-fifties and have been married for 28 years. They have three children together, one in high school and two in university. One evening, Shafee tells Kawthar that they should invite some of their friends over for dinner on the weekend. Kawthar agrees and gets down to work on the menu, planning the dinner and shopping for the necessary supplies. On Friday, the day before the dinner, Shafee tells Kawthar that he thinks she should make their favourite dish, lamb curry, for their guests tomorrow. Kawthar explains to Shafee that she already set the menu days ago and has already planned to make chicken biryani and her famous Kerala beef fry.

"But I still think lamb curry would be better. Everybody loves lamb curry," he insists.

"Yes, but I already bought all the ingredients for the chicken biryani and for the Kerala beef fry. And the dinner's tomorrow night," she replies.

"Exactly," he retorts. "There's still plenty of time to cook the lamb curry. And the grocery stores are all still open. Lots of time..." he mutters, walking out of the kitchen.

Kawthar, angry at Shafee's insensitivity, sits down at the kitchen table for a while to calm her nerves. In her head she reviews everything she still has to do before the dinner. *I still have to make all the food, bake that cake, and make the fruit salad. Plus I still have to vacuum the entire first floor...she* thinks to herself. *Where is the time to go shopping again now?* She shakes her head in frustration and resolves to continue on with her original plan so that she can get everything done in time.

Kawthar works tirelessly all Friday and Saturday, asking for some help from her children now and then, until the doorbell rings at 6pm on Saturday.

Shafee, who spent the day in his home office, emerges at the sound of the doorbell and opens the door for their guests. "Welcome, welcome." he says cheerfully. However, Shafee's happy and cheerful mood takes a downward spiral when dinner time rolls around and he realizes that Kawthar hasn't made the lamb curry he requested. He casts an annoyed look at Kawthar and makes a comment to the guests about how he "has to apologize for the dinner…" Kawthar tries her best to ignore him and enjoy her time with her guests. When it's time for dessert and Kawthar takes out the cake she's baked, the fruit salad she's made and a variety of juices and tea and coffee, Shafee looks upset once more. He runs down to the basement in a flurry and comes up with the ice cream cake they were saving for their upcoming visit to Kawthar's sister. He quickly un-wraps the cake and places it on the table with the rest of the dessert. The guests barely touch it as most of them have already served themselves from the cake Kawthar baked, and the ice cream cake sits on the table, melting away as the evening goes on.

When the last guest has finally left, Kawthar begins the daunting task of cleaning up as Shafee proceeds to remind her of "everything she did wrong".

"It was embarrassing just how empty the table looked at dessert. I couldn't bear to look at it like that, I just had to run down and bring up that ice-cream cake. You're lucky I thought of it. I don't know what we would have done without it."

Kawthar takes a deep breath and remains silent. She doesn't have the energy to argue anymore.

"And the lamb curry - or rather the missing lamb curry. Why didn't you listen to me? It would have been perfect! But nooooooo, you had to go off and do everything your way. Would it kill you to take my advice once in a while?"

Would it kill you to withhold your advice once in a while, Kawthar thinks to herself.

"Anyway, I'm going to bed" he says, and with that, he leaves Kawthar standing in the kitchen amidst a heap of dirty dishes, pots and pans and the leftover melting ice-cream cake that is quickly becoming a big puddle of goo.

As soon as he has left, Kawthar collapses on a chair in the kitchen. She has to take a few deep breaths to keep herself together. How dare he, she thinks, after all the work I put into this and every other dinner! Would a simple thank you once in a while be so hard to say!

As she sits there, she can't help but recall all the times throughout their marriage when Shafee has treated her in much the same way. In fact, it started from the very beginning of their marriage and continued into a vicious pattern. Why should she be surprised really? He's always treated her like this. And for the most part, she's always accepted this kind of treatment from him. Earlier on in the marriage, she'd put up with it for the sake of the kids. She never wanted them to see her and Shafee arguing or feel that there was disharmony at home, so she complied with Shafee's unreasonable requests just to keep him quiet. But now, she can't take it anymore. Besides, the kids are all grown up and they eventually have to see what life is really like.

She remembers when she was pregnant and longing for her mother's tender care, how Shafee wouldn't agree to let her go and stay with her parents for a bit.

"I'll leave you cooked meals in the freezer," she had pleaded.

"No," he had said, "it's not the same. I want my wife to be with me when I sit down for dinner. We're a family now. You can't just go running off to Mommy and Daddy whenever you're not feeling well. Besides, the grocery store is filled with frozen dinners; so don't make this about the food."

Then, when their first daughter Saba was born, Shafee still expected Kawthar to have the time to cook and take care of the house chores all by herself and also be good company for him. He would play with the baby at times but never offered to take care of the baby so Kawthar could get in a quick nap, even when it was so obvious that she was exhausted and lacking sleep. Kawthar tried very hard to balance her new life as a new and exhausted mother with the daily routine of life, but Shafee never seemed satisfied with what she did. The worst part was, even though he showed his dissatisfaction with their new circumstances, he never got involved to change things. She never could seem to reason with him so she often resorted to ignoring him (when she could get away with it) or passively taking his orders. But over the years, her resentment toward him has grown so strong that she doesn't think she can put up with his behaviour anymore. Enough is enough she thinks to herself as she sits there in the dead of night surrounded by dirty dishes and piles of leftover food. I will no longer allow myself to be treated like his servant! There must be a better way! This relationship needs lots of work.

Why it is inappropriate:

• Shafee waits until the day before the dinner, after Kawthar has already made certain preparations for the dinner, to come and tell Kawthar that he wants her to make lamb curry. If Shafee wanted something in particular, he should have gotten involved early enough in the planning process and should have offered to help with certain tasks, such as grocery shopping.

• On the day of the dinner, Shafee spent most of his time in his home office, even though there were many tasks to be done before their guests arrived. Shafee never offered to help Kawthar with any of the preparations. This is contrary to the example of the Prophet Mohamed *SAAW*, who was always in the service of his family. A Muslim husband should follow the example of the Prophet and always offer to help his wife because that brings a positive and healthy atmosphere to the relationship.

• During the dinner itself, Shafee makes his disappointment with Kawthar and the food very obvious by making certain demeaning comments and casting annoyed looks at Kawthar. This is contrary to the etiquettes of naseeha (advice giving), as indicated to us by the Prophet *SAAW*. Advice should be given in private and in a gentle manner. These demeaning comments and looks will only leave resentment in Kawthar's heart and mind and will have a negative impact on their marriage.

• Even after the dinner when Shafee speaks to Kawthar in private in their kitchen, he only criticizes everything he feels she did wrong. He never thanks her or shows his appreciation for all her efforts. A Muslim should always be thankful to whoever does something for him or her, as the Prophet *SAAW's* teachings state that he who does not thank people does not thank Allah *SWT*.[100] Again, after the dinner Shafee also doesn't offer to help her with cleaning up, he just stands there criticizing her.

• From the different incidents mentioned in this story, it looks like Shafee does not understand the real meaning of qawamah. Based on Kawthar's reflections, it seems that Shafee has developed a pattern of misusing his duty as a husband to be demanding and order Kawthar around, taking into consideration only his own desires and wants. He seldom consults with her on any matters related to the family and does not take her needs into consideration. For example, when she was pregnant and after the baby was born, Shafee's only concern was that his wife should be around him at home, neglecting her need to rest and be cared for by her family.

Note: By being passive and accepting this kind of treatment from their husbands, many wives contribute to the development of the negative pattern in the relationship. This is evident in Kawthar's case, as she was putting up with this sort of behaviour from Shafee since the beginning of their marriage, without discussing with him how it made her feel or how it affected their relationship. It would have been much more appropriate to communicate to Shafee that their relationship should be built on respect, communication and consultation early enough in the marriage. If she had done this and not allowed this pattern to continue to build over time, she could have avoided the overwhelming resentment that she now feels toward Shafee, which is very unhealthy for the marriage.

---

[100] At-Termizy

Arabic Terminology

INTRODUCTION

In most Islamic books, there are Arabic terms that are frequently used throughout. These words generally constitute basic religious vocabulary that needs to be available to the reader. In the following glossary of Arabic terms, we attempt to provide most of the terms used in this book with their definitions. Some of the terms may have not been used in this book; however, we have decided to include them in this glossary for the readers' general benefit.

GLOSSARY OF ARABIC TERMS

TERM	DEFINITION
Adhan	The call for prayer
Ahadeeth	The collection of the sayings of Prophet Muhammad *SAAW*
Ajr	Reward from Allah for doing the right thing
Al Asmaa `al Husna	The beautiful attributes of Allah
Al Fatihah	The first chapter of **Quràn**
Al Mustaqeem	The Upright, or the Straight
Al Qayoom	The One Who sustains and protects all that exists
Al Fawahish	Shameful deeds
Ansar	Supporters, usually refering to the Muslims of the city of Madinah who supported the prophet *SAAW*

Aqeedah	Islamic creed
Athkar	Plural of *Thikr*, which refers to the remembrance of Allah through words, meditation, and reflection
Da'wah	Call or mission. It usually refers to calling others to follow Allah's way.
Deen	A way of life. It is usually used for the religion of Islam.
Derham	An old currency used by Arabs made of silver or copper. It has a lesser value than a Dinar.
Dinar	An old valuable golden currency used by Arabs.
Dua'a	Supplication
Eid	The Muslim celebration after the month of Ramadan and/or during the pilgrimage
Fahishah	Shameful or obscene deed
Fajr	Dawn. It usually applies to the first obligatory prayer of the day, whose time extends from dawn until sunrise.
Fetnah	Temptation
Fiqh	The ability to understand and derive rules and regulations from existing texts and evidence for practical Islamic applications and regulations related to the immediate environment
Gelbab	A loose, one-piece dress that cover the whole body

Golab Jamen	A famous sweet dish common in the Indian sub-continent
Hadeeth	Reports of the prophet's sayings, actions, and approval
Hadramout	A region along the south coast of the Arabian Peninsula
Hajr	To distance oneself from something or to avoid something
Halal	Allowed or permitted according to Islam
Halaqa	Circle. Usually refers to a study circle
Haram	Forbidden or prohibited according to Islam
Hijab	Muslim women's proper dress. It covers every thing except the face and hands. It could take any form as long as it meets the requirements of being non-transparent and loose so it doesn't describe the body detail
Ibadah	Any act of worship
Ihsan	The process of perfecting your deeds. According to the hadeeth of the prophet *SAAW*, it is to worship Allah as if you see Him, and if you don't see Him, He sees you.
Ihssun	To provide immunity. In the marriage context, it refers to the process of ensuring that people are protected through marriage from resorting to illicit means to fulfill their sexual desires

Insha'a Allah	God willing
Iman	Believing
Imam	A Muslim Religious leader or a Muslim who leads the congregational prayers. It is also used to refer to the head of an Islamic school of thought (*Mathhab*) like Imam Malik, Ahmad, Al Shafei, and Abu Hanifah
Iqamah	To establish
Isha	The fifth Islamic prayer of the day. Usually it is an hour and a half after sunset, depending on the geographical location.
Istekhara	To seek advice from Allah via a specific prayer to guide you to make the right decision regarding any issue
Istiqamah	to remain upright and steadfast, facing all difficulties and hardships
Itekaf	Seclusion. Usually it refers to the act of staying in the mosque for a longer time than the time of the prayers with the purpose of worship. Although it can be done at any time, it is practiced more by Muslims during the month of Ramadan.
Jannah	Paradise
Jumuàh	Friday. There is a special congregational prayer for Muslims on this day

Kabab	A famous meat dish common in the Middle East
Khatib	The one who delivers Friday sermon
Khimar	A large, loose one-piece scarf that covers a lady's head as well as her shoulders and may reach down to her waist
Khutbah	The speech (sermon) delivered during Friday congregational prayer
Kursi	The general meaning is chair. However, in a religious context, it is used to refer to the Throne of God
Masjid	Mosque
Mawadah	One of the two most important foundations on which marriage in Islam is based. It emphasizes a deeper sense of love, wonderful communication, and kind treatment. The other element is *Rahmah*, which implies kindness, compassion, and leniency.
Miswak	A small part of the branch of a special tree that was used as a tooth brush by early Muslims
Mo'ahadah	To enter into an agreement, to sign a contract, or to make a pledge.
Mo'aqabah	The process of punishing yourself for committing mistakes that should have been avoided

Mohasabah	The process of reviewing, assessing, and evaluating your deeds regularly to ensure that they are as close to Allah's orders as possible
Mojahadah	The process of striving hard to be your best in everything you do
Moraqabah	The process of observing your duties toward Allah and of feeling that He is with you at all times
Motaqeen	Those who observe their duties toward Allah
Nafl	Extra. Usually it refers to an extra act of worship over the obligatory and the Sunnan that a Muslim may volunteer to do on his own to get closer to Allah
Nawafel	Plural of *Nafl*
Niqab	Cover over the face of a lady.
Nushooz	Comes from the verb nashaza, meaning ("It became raised" or "it rose"). The technical or legal meaning of the term nushooz is when each spouse transgresses, treats the other in an improper manner, and is hostile towards the other
Qawamah	A degree of responsibility and authority that Allah gave to men to take full care of women's maintenance and protection and to spend from their possessions on women. It implies no superiority or advantage before the law. The man's role

of leadership in relation to his family does not mean that husbands hold a dictatorship over their wives. Although this degree of *Qawamah* gives men the authority to make the final decision in matters related to family, it also entrusts them with the responsibility to consult their wives and to provide protection and maintenance to the family in the best possible way.

Qiyam al Layl	To stand up for prayer at night
Quràanic	Related to **Qur'an**
Rahmah	Kindness, compassion, and leniency
Ramadan	The ninth month of the Islamic calendar. Muslim are supposed to fast from dawn to sunset during this month.
Sakan	A place of dwelling. In the marriage context, it implies the inclination of spouses to each other and the mutual comfort they should provide to each other on the physical as well as the emotional level
Salaf	The generation of the early Muslims who came after the generation of the companions of the prophet *SAAW* and the generation that followed them
Salah	Prayer
Sana'a	A city in the southwest of the Arabian Peninsula, now the capital of Yemen.

Seerah	The biography of the life of Prophet Muhammad *SAAW*
Selat al rahem	The act of being kind to our blood relatives
Shaqae'q	Equivalent to each other
Shaytan	The devil
Sunnah	Way, teaching, or guidance. In the Islamic con text, it always refers to the guidance provided to Muslims by Prophet Muhammad SAAW
Sunnan	Plural of Sunnah
Surat/Surah	Qur'anic chapter
Tafseer	Explanation or the interpretation of the **Qur'an**
Tarbiyah	The art of dealing with human nature with guidance and providing the right direction in order to better people
Taraweeh	A special prayer after Isha during the nights of the month of Ramadan
Taqwa	Being always aware of our duties towards Allah and trying to shield our selves from His punishment by fulfilling our religious duties and avoiding sins
Tawaf	To go in circles around the Ka'bah
Tawfeeq	Success

Tazkeiah	The process of purification. Usually it is used for soul purification via extra acts of worship and remembrance of Allah
Tazkiatu Annafs	The process of the purification of the soul
Thikr	Remembering Allah and mentioning Him
Ummah	Community
Waleemah	The meal served to guests on the occasion of marriage. It is a Sunnah to slaughter a sheep or a lamb on such an occasion and use its meat to prepare food for the guests.
Wudu	Ablution, or the act of cleaning oneself in a specific way by washing certain parts of the body to be ready for prayer
Yawm al-Qiyamah	The day when the dead will be raised from their graves and all of them will stand up before Allah
Zakah	The meaning of the word is growth. The religious terminology is "obligatory charity"

References

1. ———. *The Noble Qur'an, English Translation of the Meanings and Commentary.* Medina, Kingdom of Saudi Arabia: King Fahd Complex for the Printing of the Holy Qur'an, 1417 A.H.

2. Al Alammah Ahmad Ibn Muhammad Ibn Aly Almaqry Al faiomy. *Ketab AlMesbah Al Muneer Fi Ghareeb Al Sharh Al Kabeer,* Part 1 and 2, Six edition, *Al-Matbah Al Amereiah, Cairo, 1925*

3. Al Allamah Ahmad Ibn Muhammad Ibn Aly Al Fayoomy al Maqrey, *Al Mesbah Al Muneer, 1st edition,* Contemporary Library for printing and publications, Saida, Beirut, 1417H, 1996

4. Nadeem Mara'shly and Osama Mara'shly, *Al-Saheeh Fi Alloghah Wa Aloloom, Dar Alhadarah Al-Arabiah,* Beirut, first edition, 1975

5. Majd Al Deen Al Fayrooz Abady, *Al Qamoos al Moheet*, Vol. 3 page 168, Al-Sa'adah Print house, Egypt, 1913, 1332H

6. Aby Al Fadl Jamal al Deen Muhammad Ibn Makram Ibn Manzoor Al-Afriqey Al-Masry*, Lesan al Arab* Volume 12, Sader House for Printing and Publications, Beirut, 1956, 1375H

7. Al Mo'alem Botros al Bostany, *Qamoos Motawwal for Arabic Language; Moheet al Moheet,* Maktabat Lobnan, Reyad al Solh square, Beirut, 1987

8. Abdur Rasheed Sidddiqui, *Qur'anic Keywords, A Reference Guide,* The Islamic Foundation, United Kingdom, 2008

9. Mohammad Asad, *The message of the Qur'an Translated and Explained,* Dar Al-Andalus, Gibraltar, second edition 1984.

10. *The Qur'an, Anew Translation* by M. A. S. Abdel Haleem, Oxford University Press Inc., New York, 2004

11. Dr. Mohammad Mohsen Khan and Dr. Mohammad Taqi-ud-din Al Hilali, *Interpretation of The Meaning of The Nobel Qur'an in English language*, Part 1, first edition, 1989, Kazi Publications, Lahor, Pakistan

12. Maulana Abdul Majid Dayrabadi, *Holy Qur'an with English Translation and Commentary* , Vol 1, The Taj Company Ltd., Karachi, Pakistan

13. Dr. Ahmad Zidan, Mrs. Dina Zidan, *The Glorious Qur'an, Text and Transalation,* Islamic Home, Publishing and Distribution, 1996, Cairo, Egypt.

14. Muhammad M. Pickthall, *The Meaning of The Glorious Qur'an, Text and Explanatory Translation*, Muslim World League, Mecca Al-Mukarramah Saudi Arabia, 1977

15. Zafar Ishaq Ansari, *Towards Understanding the Qur'an,* Vol.II, Surah 4-6, *English Version of Tafhim al-Qur'an* by Syyid Abul A'la Mawdudi, The Islamic Foundation, Leicester, United Kingdom 1989

16. Abdallah Yusuf Ali, *The Holy Qur'an, Translation and Commentary,* Published by American Trust Publications for The Muslim Students' Association of the United States and Canada. 2nd Edition, June 1977

17. T. B. Irving (Al-Hajj Ta'lim A'li), *The Qur'an, the Noble reading, Translation and Commentary,* 1993, The Mother Mosque Foundation, Cedar Rapids, Iowa, USA

18. Muhammad Al-Jibaly *The Muslim Family-3 The Fragile Vessels,*, Al-Kitaab and as Sunnah Publishing, Arlington Texas, 2000

19. Ahmed Ali *Al Qur'an–A Contemporary Translation,* Princeton University Press, 41 William St. Princeton, New Jersey, fifth printing, 1994

20. Aby Alqasem Al-Husain Muhammad known as Raghib Al-Asfahany, *Al Mufradat fi Ghareeb Al-Qur'an.* Dar Alma'refah lel-tebaa'h wal Nashr, Beirut, Lebanon

21. Aby Abdallah Muhammad ben Ahmad Al-Ansary al-Qortoby, *Al-Jame' Le-Ahkam Al-Qur'an*, Arabic writer's House for printing and publications, Cairo, 1967

22. Sheikh Muhammad Ali Assabony, *Rawae'e Al-Bayan Tafseer Aayaat Al Ahkaam,* Vol one, Maktabat Al Ghazaly, Damascus, Syria, third print 1400 H, 1980

23. Aby Al-Fadl Shehab Al-Deen Al-Sayed Mahmood Al-Aloosy Al-Baghdady, *Rooh Al-Ma'any fi Tafseer Al-Qur'an Al-A'zeem Walsabe' Al-Mathany,* Part 5, Dar Ihyaa' Al-Torath Al-A'raby, Beurutt, Lebanon.

24. Muhammad Ali Assabony, *Mukhtasar Tafseer Ibn Katheer,* Dar Al Qur'an Al Kareem, Beirut, Lebanon, 1402 H, 1981. Vol. 1

25. Mohammad Al-Razy Fakhr Al Deen, *Tafseer Al Fakhr Al Razy* Vol. 9, Dar Al Fekr for printing, publishing and distribution

26. Dr. Wahbah Al-Zaihaily, *Al-Tafseer Al-Muneer fi Alaqeedah wal-Sharee'ah wal Manhaj,* Vol. 5, Dar Al-Fekr, Damascus, Syria

27. Dr. Abdulhamid A. Abusulayman, **Marital Discord, Recapturing the Islamic Spirit of Human Dignity,** The International Institute of Islamic Thought, 2003, Herndon, VA, USA

28. Sayyid Qutb, **In The Shade Of The Qur'an, Fi Zilal al Qur'an,** Translated and edited by Adil Salahi & Ashur Shamis, Vol. 3 2001/1421H, The Islamic Foundation

29. Muhammad Jamal Al-Qasemy, **Tafseer Al-Qasemy, Mahasen Al-Ta'weel,** Chapter 5, Dar Ihyaa, Al-Kutob Al-A'rabiah, Cairo, Egypt

30. Abdel Haleem Abu Shoqah, **Tahreer Al-Mara'h Fi Asr Al Resalah,** Vol. 5, The place of women in the family. Dar Al Qalam for publications and Distribution, Kwait,

31. Dr. Saalih ibn Ghaanim Al-Sadlaan, **Marital Discord (al-Nushooz).** Al-Basheer publications and Translations, Translated by Jamaal al-Din M. Zarabozo, 1996

32. Imam Abi Al-Husain Muslim Ibn Al-Haggag Al-Qushairee Al-Naisabouree. **Sahih Muslim,** first edition. Cairo: Dar Ihiaa' Alkutob Alarabia, 1955.

33. Imam Abi Abdellah Muhammad Ibn Ismail Ibn Ibraheem Ibn Al-Mogheirah Ibn Bardezabah Al-Bukhari. **Sahih al-Bukhari,** Cairo, *Dar Al Shaa'b.*

34. Imam Al-Hafez Abi Dawud Sulaiman Ibn Al-Asha'th Al-Sagestany Al-Azdei. **Sunan Aby Dawud,** first edition. Beirut, *Dar Ibn Hazm,* 1998.

35. Imam Al-Hafez Aby Abderahaman Ahmad Ibn Shua'ib Ibn Ali Ibn Senan Ibn Dinar Al-Nisa'i. *Sunan Al-Nisa'i,* first edition. Beirut, Dar Ibn Hazm, 1999.

36. Imam Ibn Majah. *Sunan Ibn Majah,* first edition. Cairo, Dar Ihiaa'At Turath Al-A'raby, 1975.

37. Imam Malik Ibn Anas. *Mowata' Al Imam Malek*, ninth edition. Beirut, Dar Al-Nafae's, 1985. Prepared by Ahmad Rateb Armoosh.

38. Other books of *Hadith, Ahmad, Tabarani, Tirmidhi,* and so on.

39. Okasha Abdel Mannan al Tayiby, *Women in the Shade of the Qur'an, Arabic,* Al Fadeelah House for publications, distribution, and exporting, 1992. Cairo, Egypt.

40. Dr. Yusuf Al Qaradawi, *The Place of Women in Islamic life,* Arabic, Al-Resalah Establishment, Beirut, Lebanon, 2000

41. Omar al Telmesany, *Islam and its Noble Position on Women,* Arabic, Islamic distributing and publishing house, 1990, Cairo, Egypt,

42. Dr. Hasan al Turaby, *Women between the Teachings of the Religion and Practices of the Society,* Arabic, Saudi house for publishing and Distribution 1984, Jeddah, Saudi Arabia

43. Hussein Muhammad Yousof, *Selection of spouses in Islam and Courting Etiquettes,* Arabic, Dar al Ee'tesam, 1979, Cairo, Egypt

44. Abdallah Naseh Elwan, ***Polagmy in Islam and the Wisdom That the Prophet SAAW Had More Than One Wife,*** Arabic, Dar al-Salaam for printing, publishing, distributing, and Translation, third edition, 1986, Cairo, Egypt.

45. Ruqaiyyah Waris Maqsood, ***The Muslim Marriage Guide,*** Goodword Books, 2002, New Delhi, India

46. Jameelah Jones and Abu Ameenah Bilaal Philips, ***The Rational and Laws Behind Plural Marriage in Islam,*** International Islamic Publishing House, 1987, Riyadh, Saudi Arabia

47. M. El-Sayem, ***The Rights of The Husband and Wife,*** Islamic Book Services, Branford, NJ, USA

48. Dr. Ahmed H. Sakr, ***Matrimonial Education in Islam,*** Foundation of Islamic Knowledge, 1991, Lombard, IL, USA.

49. Sajda Nazlee, ***Feminism and Muslim Women,*** Ta-Ha Publishers Ltd., 1996, London, United Kingdom

50. Dr. Hasan al Turaby, ***Women in Islam and Muslim Society,*** Milestones (London) Publishers, 1991

51. Dr. Gamal A. Badawi, ***Polygamy in Islamic Law,*** The Muslim Student Associations of the USA and Canada, third printing, 1976, Maryland, USA

52. Maulana Wahiduddin Khan, ***Women between Islam and Western Society,*** Goodword Books, 1995, New Delhi, India.

53. Dr. Yusuf Al Qaradawi, ***The Status of Women in Islam,*** Islamic Home Publishing and Distributing, 1997, Cairo, Egypt

54. Dr. Jamal Badawi, *The Muslim Woman's Dress According to The Qur'an and Sunnah,* Ministry of Awqaf and Islamic Affairs, Kuwait

55. Al-Ghazaly, Shaykh Muhammad, *Qadaia Al-Mara'h bayna al Taqaleed al-Rakedah, eal Wafedah,* Dar al Shorook, third edition, 1991, Cairo Egypt.

56. S haykh Abel Muta'al al Jabry, *Al-Mara'h fi al Tasawor al Islami,* Arabic, Maktabat Wahbah, Second edition, 1976, Cairo, Egypt

57. Badriah al Azzaz, *Almara'h, maza ba'da al Soqoot,* Arabic, *Maktabat al Mannar al Islamiah,* second Edition, 1988, Kuwait

58. Dr. Abdel Haleem Mahmoud, *Al Mara'h al Muslimah wa Fiqh al-Da'wah ela Allah,* Arabic, Alwafa' for printing and publishing, 1990, Al-Mansourah, Egypt

59. Al-Ghazaly, Shaykh Muhammad, *Nahwa Tafseer Madooe'y Lesewar Al-Qur'an Al-Kareem,* Arabic, seventh edition, Dar Al-Shrooq, Cairo, Egypt

60. Sh. Muhammad Al-Ghazaly, *A Thematic Commentary on The Qur'an,* Vol. I, page 63, Translated by Ashur A. Shamis, International Institute of Islamic Thought, Herndon, Virginia, USA, 1420AH/1999AC

61. Jerald F. Dirks, *The Abrahamic Faiths, Judaism, Christianity, and Islam, Similarities & Contrasts,* amana publications Beltsville, Maryland, USA, 2004